When The Dealers Robbed
Vegas....And Other Tales

When The Dealers Robbed Vegas....And Other Tales

Based on A True Story

*To, Anita & Randy
my favorite Port
Time neighbors,
8-5-17*

NEAL LIOSI

The names and places have been changed to protect the innocent and the guilty. Any correlation to actual people and/or places is strictly coincidental.

@ Copyright 2017 by Neal Liosi

ISBN: 1545234639
ISBN 13: 9781545234631
Library of Congress Control Number: 2017907259
CreateSpace Independent Publishing Platform
North Charleston, South Carolina

All rights reserved. No part of this publication may be reproduced, stored in retrieval system, or transmitted, in any form or by any means, electronic, mechanical, photocopying, recording, or otherwise, without written permission of the publisher. Printed in the United States of America.

Dedicated to All the Craps Dealers in Las Vegas

Contents

	Foreward · ix
One	Breaking In · 1
Two	Downtown ·17
Three	Flamingo - The Hustle · · · · · · · · · · · · ·35
Four	The Agent ·49
Five	MGM – The Crew · · · · · · · · · · · · · · · ·71
Six	MGM - The Agent Returns · · · · · · · · · ·93
Seven	Four Queens, Paradise And Royal LV · · 105
Eight	Salvatories · 121
Nine	Drugs – The End · · · · · · · · · · · · · · · · · 135

The Author and Dealer – Neal Liosi.

Foreward

"The City is Wide Open": That was the call I got back in 1968 from my brother, Paulie. That phone call changed my life forever. He knew me and he knew the skills I had. I was just 22 years old living in Cleveland. Living anywhere else was extremely attractive to me. Back in the sixties, Cleveland was an extension of Pittsburgh. There was smoke and grime constantly in the air. It was industry at its worst. And, the winters were unbearable. So, when I got that call, I was all too eager to go. I knew living in Cleveland was a dead end, so, I packed my stuff and drove my VW across the country with only four hundred dollars in my pocket. But after that short conversation with my brother, I knew I would be successful. It was an environment for the taking. I was good at taking.

Back in the sixties, the Mob was running Vegas. Okay, Hughes came on the scene as well but make no mistake about it, the Mob was running things even at Howard Hughes places. Somehow though, the Mob, they had their own set of rules about territory. Each different casino reported back to a different family back East. They did not interfere with each other because everybody was making money. So why screw up a good thing? I would see the bag man come in every so often to the count room. He was in and he was out. I kept my head down. It was none of my business. The Mob consisted of pretty sharp people. They had a hundred percent upside on everything. They talked the Teamsters Union into putting up the money to buy the casino. So, there was no money out of the Mob's pocket. Then the Goodfellas would help themselves to the skim once to twice a month. Free money.

Well, the skim accomplished a few things. First, it lowered the profits of the Casino, so there was less taxes to be paid to the Federal Government. Plus, when the casinos were losing money, which is improbable at best but happened all of the time, the Teamsters Pension Fund could not afford to have their investment go belly up, so what did they do? They put more money in to save their investment. It was brilliant. The Mob had no money in the operation and the poor blue collar worker working 8 hour days, everyday, was paying into the Pension Fund which went to hold the Casinos afloat which went to the Mob. It was a tax free event with no risk of capital. Brilliant! But this is old news.

The Mob wasn't the only ones robbing the casinos. We were! The Dealers! Instead of one guy going in the count room once or twice a month, we were there every day stealing. They did not see us coming. To this day they do not know what hit them. There were hundreds of us. And we were all doing it. It took a lot of skill and guts. Because not only were you ripping off the Casino, you were indirectly ripping off the Mob and they do not like being ripped off. But we did it anyway. Not only did we rob the casinos, we hustled every customer we could. We had techniques and had people in the business who developed schemes only true thieves could devise. These people (dealers) could be in any high level management job out there. The schemes we came up with were brilliant, innovative, and time tested.

Robbing and stealing has to be in your blood. Just like being a gangster. You just can't become a gangster. It has to be in your blood. You have to love being a gangster. We loved being thieves. If we could steal it, we would. It was a wild time. Vegas was wide open and we were there. When I got the phone call, I couldn't wait to get in the action. The following stories tells how we did it, the schemes we used, the money we got, who we got it from, the celebrities, the drugs, the great times and the bad times. This book describes "When the Dealers Robbed Vegas and other Tales". And they're all true!

Breaking in Downtown.

One

BREAKING IN

It was 1968. I was 22 years old and I was going through a divorce. I needed some down time so my Brother, Paulie Porkchops, called me and suggested I go out to Vegas for a vacation. We called him Porkchops because he was pretty well built due to all the time he would spend at the gym. While I was there, he told me how quick it was to get a divorce in Vegas. Back in those days in Cleveland, you had to wait two years to get a divorce. In Vegas, you could get a divorce in only six short weeks! That was unheard of anywhere else in the country. He told me: "Look Neal, come out here and I can teach you how to deal craps. In no time you'll have a job. This place is like a second chance." I watched him come home from work emptying his pockets with more cash and chips than I ever saw. He would take me out to many of the bars and restaurants in town. This was all new to me. The place was exciting and I was excited.

After the vacation, I went back to Cleveland. It was cold as can be and snowing every other day. It was miserable. I had a day job as a machinist. It was a boring, drudgery job. I would go in each day through the cold and snow thinking about my time in Nevada. I was thinking I should have never left. I needed a new, fresh start. Shortly thereafter, my Brother called me to check in. He said: "Hey Neal, the City is Wide Open out here! You can come out here and stay with me if you want. Before you know it, you'll be divorced, a free man, and have a new life." It really didn't take long for me to think about it. I went to the machinist union and asked to borrow $400. They gave it to me. It was the last they saw of me and the last time they saw their $400.

I packed what personal stuff I had and loaded my Volkswagen Bug. I headed out the next day driving south to St. Louis, the gateway to the west. There I picked up the famous Route 66. I was so excited, I just kept on driving. My original plan was to sleep in the car on the way out but I just kept driving. Just my luck, outside of Saint Louis, the VW broke down. I popped open the hood, looked at the engine and saw a cotter pin had broken off which helps the carburetor operate. I didn't know what to do miles away by myself with a broken down car and only $400 in my pocket. I searched around the car for something which could help. I found an old bobby pin left in the car from my soon-to-be ex. I put the bobby pin where the cotter was and hoped for the best. I couldn't believe it held and I was back up and running. I got back to my journey. Do you believe when I sold the car years later, that pin was still in the glove compartment waiting to save me again?

In those days, Route 66 led you through many towns that simply existed for the highway. When you were not going through a town, you were driving in pure, open, vast country. You could look for miles and see nothing but grass and some mountains in the distance. The wind in the plains was so strong and gusty, it blew my VW all over the road. I was scared and excited all at the same time. I tried to sleep in the car but couldn't do it. So, I just kept driving. I made it to Vegas in a little less than 48 hours. I was beat, but I made it. My Brother and his wife welcomed me to move into their house. I made it and my life was about to change!

In no time, Pauli got me an interview with the "Shill Boss" at the Fremont Casino downtown. In those days, everybody who wanted to deal had to start downtown. It was the unwritten rule. The "Shill Boss" was a white guy with blond hair about in his forties. He had this gaunt, ghostly look about him. He was thin and it appeared the desert had sucked out most of the moisture from his body. If you look around these days, you can still see them. They are the people who grew up here. You can just pick them out. Most of them are Mormons like he was. In fact, Vegas is mostly based with Mormons. Howard Hughes surrounded himself with them. They tend to work hard, not drink when together, and are quiet. Similar to the Quakers back east. The Boss and I sat down for 15 minutes. He was giving me an interview as a favor for my Brother. My brother had a lot of connections around town.

"So" he says. "What do you want to do?" I told him I wanted to deal craps like my brother. My brother put up a four by eight foot table in one of his bedrooms so he could teach me. He put a craps layout green felt on it. So, thinking I had a pretty good mentor to teach me, I thought craps was a good entry point. The "Shill Boss" looked at me quietly for a few minutes, leaned forward with a straight face and said: "Okay kid. Come back tonight with a white shirt on and black trousers. Tell the Floor Boss you need to see me." I came back later that night all fluffed and buffed with the outfit he told me to wear. I was ready!

I wasn't quite sure what the "Shill Boss" did but I would find out quickly. In order to "Break In", you first had to work downtown and you first had to be a "Shill". I had no idea what it was but was soon to find out. The Boss came over to me and told me to stand by this pole which was behind the tables. "Listen kid, your job for right now is to play at the dead games on twenty one and craps tables. This is what I am going to do. I am going to clap my hands and point to a table. What you do, is walk over to that table and start playing. The dealer is going to give you ten chips. You bet only one at a time and no more until I tell you to leave the table. If you run out of chips we will stake you another ten chips. Any questions?" I said "No". Of course this did not make any sense to me. I was to stand at this pole until the Boss told me to go to a table and gamble with the House's money on one of their tables until I was told to stop. I was confused but I did what I was told.

It did not take long and sure enough he clapped and pointed to a twenty one game. You always went to a dead table. A dead game is one where no one is playing. I sat down. The dealer winked at me and gave me ten chips. I sat there a little confused. The dealer then looked at me and said: "Well, are you going to place a bet? Remember just one chip at a time." I did and I sat there playing, betting one chip at a time. I would win some hands and lose others. The losing hands started to outnumber the winning hands and I started to understand some of the concepts keeping the house ahead. Before you know it, a few other players would sit down. Once two or three players would get in the game, the dealer would look at me and give a nod. At first I didn't know what he was doing. After a few nods I figured out he wanted me to leave the table and go back to the pole. I gave the dealer the remaining chips and I reported back to the pole. While there, I kept my eye on the "Shill Boss" to see where he wanted me to go next.

Shortly, I would hear another clap and look to the Boss who would point to a crap table. There was only one player playing. He was not really playing much and just seemed to be leaning on the table holding his chips refusing to be the come out roller. I walked up and the dealer spotted me ten chips. I placed one on the pass line. The stick man pushed five dice my way. I selected two dice and I threw them towards the other end of the table. The dice came out as a seven. The stick man who controls the game said loudly: "Winner Seven". Beginner's luck I guess. I soon realized the stickman controls the game by controlling the dice and by giving the play by play announcements of the dice rolled. I could not roll again until he pushed the dice to me. I threw again. This time the dice came out as a six. I learned quickly in order to have a successful roll, you need to hit sixes and eights. The point was six. The next roll was a five. The stickman spoke up: "Five, five, No field five". I had no idea what he was talking about! The next roll was a six. The stick man pronounced: "Winner Six, pay the line, take the dont's".

The next thing you know, people would start to move towards the table. At first they would just look.

Then the customers would start taking money out of their pockets, and place it on the green felt in order to get chips. They did it in a quick fashion as if they were about to miss out on something. Once some people would flow to the game, more people would flow to the game. The boxman would look and me, nod, and at this point I knew I needed to return to the pole. Before you knew it, the table was full.

I learned the first two rules about craps: First, a customer never walks up to a dead game. There needs to be action to attract a player and the more players, the more desire for people to play the game. The second rule was never to play at a game which just opened up. The new dice, believe it or not, have sharp edges to them. They tend to hit and stick. Plus it always seemed like the dice for a new game were always ice cold. People want to get on a game which is in progress. One where the edges are worn down and the dice roll freely.

After that first event, I finally figured out what I was doing. I was the "Shill"! A "Shill" is basically a plant by the casino to get action going on a "dead game" – a game with no one playing. Once two to three people would show up, I would get the nod and I would go back to the pole. Do you know this method worked every time! For some reason, and especially with the craps table, people are adverse to playing, unless there are people on the table playing already. Crap Players are really superstitious about tables with no players. They think the table went cold and everyone left. Plus, they want a variety of players so if one shooter is unlucky, there may be a lucky shooter up next. So the "Shill", me, would get action going on the table and then duck out once it was up and running. It worked. It worked every time.

I was getting paid $15 a shift to stand at the pole. You would not share in any tips from the table. The dealers kept them. I would get a check every week for $60 less taxes. In order to be a dealer, you normally had to break in this way. All new dealers had to work as the "Shill" first. At the time I was trying to break in, there were about five other guys doing the same thing. These guys came out here from all over the country. They all seemed to have some family member they were living with temporarily or some of the guys would hook up and share a place. Fifteen bucks was not a lot of money. Meaning, you couldn't live on it. You had to budget the best you could.

All the new guys needed someone to help support them. In my case it was my brother, Paulie. He helped me out with housing. Still, I needed to eat, and I tried to eat as cheap as I could. The Fremont Casino had a meal special called the "Dealer's Special". Today, these type of meal specials are extinct. You know the steak and eggs special for $1.99. Today, it has to be between 2 am and 3 am on Tuesday while standing on your head and it is $9.99!! Back then, the "Dealer's Special" was 69 cents at the counter in the casino. You got two eggs, hash browns, choice of breakfast meat, toast, and coffee. It was a **REAL** special. Most of us would eat at the counter three times a day. Normally you would eat by yourself during a break. There were other specials as well which involved alcohol but at this point for me it was strictly cheap food to get me through the day. The other specials would come later and come often. It was part of the profession.

At this point, I worked the pole at night and during the day I would go to dealer school with the other guys. The school was six weeks long. It cost $150. The school was located upstairs in one of the hotel rooms. There were a few crap tables there and we could practice anytime we wanted. But guess who taught the school? **The "Shill Boss".** We would pay him $25 a week. Now keep in mind we were only making $60 a week. So, he was taking almost half of our pay. And guess where that money went? That's right! Right into his pocket. He had a pretty good thing going on.

After a few weeks, I noticed him write something down in a control book. One day, when no one was around, I looked in the drawer to find the book and what was in it. Turns out, each time one of us would pay him, he would write us down as being paid for that week. Now, he received payment at different intervals. Some guys might be behind a week or so and other guys would pay on time as they go. Whenever someone paid him, he would mark it down in his book. Frankly, I got tired of paying him half of my check each week. So, when he was not around, I would get the book out of the desk and mark me down as paid for that week. I did it three times so I basically, I gave myself a 50% discount. I thought this was pretty smart of me. It worked and it was just the start of things to come.

Thankfully, Paulie was really experienced at craps. So, when I was not working or in dealer school, he would teach me at his house. He had the whole set up. He would drill the odds and payouts into me over and over again. He would actually yell at me like the noise in the casino. Craps is tough to learn. There are all sorts of different payouts and there is noise and people yelling out to you with bets and a fast movement pace. You have to place and pay out quickly and accurately. After several weeks of school and my brother teaching me, and being a shill, I started to catch on. I had a good basic knowledge but I was still working the pole.

Back then, and especially Downtown back then, it was common for dealers to call out sick. After all, most of these guys were degenerate gamblers and alcoholics themselves. For some reason, this profession attracts those type of people. We were constantly having problems with people not showing up for work. And this was before cocaine hit town. Coke was only a few short years away. And when it hit town, well, we will get into that later.

One day, I was working the pole doing my Shill routine. It seemed like we were short on dealers. Suddenly, the "Shill Boss", as the boxman, yelled at me and said: "Liosi, get on the Stick". This was a different type of pole. He was telling me to be the Stickman. I was going to be the Pole, the guy who stands in the middle of the table with a stick and controls the dice which controls the game. This job had a couple of names such as the Pole, Mop or Stick. We normally called it the Pole. Many people today call it the stickman.

I was never so nervous in my life. I was scared to death. Yes, I had plenty of practice but this was real and it was real money. This was my chance! The next thing you know chips were flying from everywhere, "five dollars on the hard eight, give a "c and e" for ten, four dollars on the horn, I want ten dollars on the hard four, another guy yelling two dollars on the "c and e", one dollar "yo" for the dealers, I want fresh dice, shooters ready". I was dizzy with confusion. There were ten people yelling and hollering at me and throwing chips in my direction. It was a Saturday night and the busiest night of the week. My job was to determine who threw in the bet, place it for them, arrange it in the box so I knew who made it so there was a match up, control the dice, try to slow things down so the other dealers would catch up on their bets, and then push the bones to the shooter. Next roll: "Eleven". I said it! I gathered the dice towards me. More bets were thrown my way and I paid off the "e" bets at sixteen for one proper. I got what they call the "totals" right. Just then the "Floor Boss" walked over and spoke to the Boxman who was the "Shill Boss", and I heard him say, "You are pretty good at teaching these new kids what to do".

I Broke In! I was never so nervous in my life. But with every roll of the dice I started to gain more confidence. My hands were soaked and wet with sweat. I knew some of the regular customers and they were testing me and I was performing. I started to call out the numbers more robustly. I finally broke in. After twenty minutes someone tapped me on the shoulder and told me to move over to a new position. I was still a Rookie but I was just passed over to 2nd Base. That is the position on the right hand side of the Boxman. The rotation goes from the pole to 2nd base, right side of Boxman, to 3rd base, left side of Boxman, and then to break. Wow, I was in the game and I learned one important thing along the way! The money is in customer's pockets, on the table, in the drop box, in the tip box, in the cage, and in the count room. That is where all the money is. Now, I just needed to figure out how to get it into my pocket now that I "broke in".

The Best Place to work Downtown – The Golden Nugget.

Two

Downtown

In the late sixties, you had to break in Downtown. That was the rule. Once you got enough experience, you could move up and eventually work down on the strip where the money and the clientele were better. Downtown had all of the degenerate gamblers, alcoholics, heroin addicts, pill poppers, criminal types, and every type of low life you could imagine. Everyone was looking to score by any means possible. It was also the purgatory for dealers who screwed up on the strip. If you were caught stealing, not showing up for work, showing up drunk, showing up high, dealing drugs, hustling, and a longer litany of problems, you were put on "Purgatory Duty" and sent downtown. That was your punishment. It usually took about two years to cleanse your record. Then they would seal your record and you could go back to work on the strip. But first, you had to do your time in purgatory, and that was Downtown.

Downtown was a place for gambling and drinking in the late sixties. There weren't even any nude dancing places. It was strictly drinking and gambling. You could drive down Fremont Street, park your car, pay the meter, and be inside at a Crap table in minutes with a comp drink in your hand. The people down on the strip were a different clientele. People on the strip would dress nice when they went out for the night to the casino for a dinner, a show, and to gamble. Downtown, you had basically racetrack types who came dressed as they were. These people were all 25 cent to five dollar rounders and grinders. Many of them were there every night playing.

Like this one guy named G.L.Vito. Normally you would think this was a normal guy. He would do the eleven o'clock news on the weekends. During the week, he would sit next to the crap table on a golf chair and write down every number called out. He only made field bets. Once he felt like there was some type of trend, he would get up off the chair, rush up to the sidebar and put a red $5 chip on the Field Bet. He did this night after night. He would always lose since the Field is a low prop bet. Plus, he would never tip or place a bet for the dealers. So, one day I decided to mess with him. When it was my turn on the pole, I would call out the numbers thrown but then, without notice, I would stop calling them aloud. Vito would jump up out of his golf chair and run over to see and ask what the number was. I got such a kick out of making him jump up and down like a see saw.

This was the type of gamblers you would find downtown. They wanted to make money and couldn't wait until the next roll. The focus was to gamble at all costs. The players couldn't get the bets down fast enough. This one time we had an old guy down at the far end of the table. He was the only guy playing. Now, this stick man was a notorious drunk. Back then, you could go on your break, and walk over to the Horseshoe and drink, come back, and get back on the game. The Horseshoe started giving out comp drinks to the customers and anybody could buy a well drink for a buck and a beer for fifty cents. Most of the dealers were going there and drinking on their break times. The only issue with this dealer is he was doing drugs and drinking and he couldn't handle it. Now, the old guy was the shooter and he threw the dice down to my end. Jimmie, on the stick, stood there frozen and didn't call out the number or reach for the dice. I said to him: "Jimmie, call out six easy". He didn't. He just stood there, so I yelled it out. The very next roll, the old guy tosses it, and it comes out a hard eight. Jimmie still didn't call anything out! I looked up and over to Jimmie and suddenly he fell backwards. He fell and plopped flat out on the ground. He was totally passed out!

The next thing I knew, the Floor Boss who saw the whole thing yelled at me and said: "Liosi, get on the pole". I quickly went over and picked the stick up off the ground, assumed the dealer position, and retrieved the dice. Then the old guy down at the end of the table yells out and asks me what the number was. I answered: "Hard Eight" and the game continued on. People continued to place the bets, the boxman continued watching the action and the floor boss kept watching us. Meanwhile, Jimmie is still laying there unconscious, stone flat on the ground! Nobody cared about him. They just cared about the game and keeping the game playing. It was like ten minutes before Metro came to pick Jimmie up off the floor. That's what it was like downtown. People were there to gamble and the casinos were there to keep the games going.

In the late sixties, all of the downtown casinos only dealt in cash. There was no such thing as "credit play". Although, we did hear over at Benny Binion's place some players would get credit. It was rare though. You just never saw a Floor Boss walk up with a marker, have a customer sign it and a dealer would advance the player cheques. We would call the chips, checks or cheques. It all meant the same thing. But, they were called checks because they were considered valid currency like an I.O.U. Over at the Horseshoe, a few people would get credit. Like this one guy from Texas who would call in. That's right, "call in" as in using the phone. This guy would come into town once in a while so we knew of him. He was such a derelict gambler. He would actually call in over the phone and place bets on the roulette table. One of the dealers with the phone would take betting instructions from him. This dealer would place chips on the numbers the guy requested. Another dealer would run the rest of the action. When there were no more bets, he would wave his hand over the table, say "no more bets" and roll the ball. Meanwhile, the dealer working the phone would hold up the phone receiver so this guy from Texas could hear the winning number. It was crazy! The Horseshoe was known for trying new innovations like this. These are the types of gamblers we got downtown. They were hard core players.

There was a lot going on in town in the late sixties. There were three big projects going up. They were the Landmark, Bonanza, and the International. These casinos brought in some big named entertainers such as Liberace, Phyllis Diller, George Burns and Elvis. Barbara Streisand was the opening act during the International Hotel Grand Opening. The hotel opened in early July. As luck will have it, the air conditioning broke down. It was over a hundred degrees outside and probably more than that inside. It didn't stop anyone from gambling. People were drenching wet from the heat but they still played. Then Elvis started his performances at the International. There were people coming from all over to see these celebrities. The money was flowing all over town. With all of these hotels going up, there was also a big need for dealers. Every casino needed dealers. So, if you had some kind of issue as a dealer, they kind of looked the other way. They needed warm bodies on the tables.

I remember I was working for about eight weeks at the Fremont, most of the time on the shill pole. However, I did break in. So, they would use me whenever someone didn't show up for work. Meanwhile, my brother, Paulie, was kicked out of the Stardust for guess what? Stealing Chips! You know the next step! He was sent to "Dealer Purgatory". He got a job at the Golden Nugget because he knew the Shift Boss, Jockey Rose. We called him Jockey because he actually was a former Jockey. Now, the Shift Boss takes care of the whole operation. All of the Floor Bosses report to him. He does all the hiring and firing so he is a pretty important guy. Jockey Rose was one of meanest people I ever met. He always had scowl on his face and talked to the dealers like they were dirt.

Working at the Golden Nugget was a pretty good gig as far as Downtown was concerned. The casinos downtown were basically the same. They were smoky, sweaty, and dingy. They were just money making machines which grinded out, day in and day out. The Golden Nugget had a western theme to it. The dealers would wear white shirts with a black straight tie which has the words "Golden Nugget" written on it. The guys over at the Horseshoe would have the same outfit except their ties had a western flare to it. Kind of like a bowtie of some sort.

One thing the G.N. had over the other joints was the stage. There was a stage which was open to the casino. There was about 50 to 60 seats surrounding the stage. Usually, there was some type of entertainment going on which was a novel idea downtown. I remember Kenny Rogers playing there. It was free to sit and listen. You just had to buy two drinks. As far I can remember, it was the only entertainment going. It wasn't until Steve Wynn bought the G.N. it went high end as it is today.

At the time, the Nugget was a decent place to work. You got paid $27.50 per day plus you got Tokes (tips) which amounted to about $17 to $20 per day. So, you had a chance to make $47.50 which was a decent amount of money back then. Working the pole at the Fremont I was making $15 per day with no tips. So, I asked my brother if he could get me a job at the Nugget. He spoke to Jockey and got me an interview. I met with Jockey Rose for the interview. He asked me two questions. Did I steal and do I do drugs? I said no. He sent me to talk to Scheduler Bill.

You have to understand back in those days, there was no such thing as a Human Resource Department. Jockey Rose was the HR Department. We never filled out an application. You just got a meet and greet with the Shift Boss. In order to get the meeting, you had to know someone. In this case, my brother already had dealings with Jockey and I got my invite. Also, keep in mind, as quickly as you get hired, you can get fired. I saw dealers get fired on the spot many times for one thing or another. I thanked Jockey and I went to see Scheduler Bill.

This guy, Scheduler Bill, was an old guy in his sixties. He had this red glow about him. The type of glow you achieve by drinking gin over the years. He gave me a W-2, told me to fill it out and bring back tonight at 8 pm. Plus he told me: "Kid, just do your job and keep yourself clean and you'll be alright".

Later, at 8 pm, I showed up. At this point, all I really got accomplished was to get on the "call list". Being on the "call list" was like being in the movie "On the Waterfront". In the movie, each day, men would show up and wait to see if their name was called out to do work. It wasn't much different here. I would show up each night at 8 pm and wait to see if Scheduler Bill would call out my name so I could work that night.

Finally, one night, Scheduler Bill was shuffling through some paperwork, pulled out the "call list", and called out my name. "Liosi! Table Number Four".

I was excited but scared at the same time. The Nugget just put in a 25 cent game. I knew it was on table number four. A 25 cent table means the table will be packed with players. There will be a lot of place bets and plenty of prop bets. Plus you could expect plenty of pressing of bets. Because it was a cheap 25 cent game, everybody at the table is going to be making some kind of prop bet. So, if you are going to learn the game of craps down cold, there is no better place than a 25 cent game. And since most of these players are regulars, they will spot every mistake you make and make a big deal about it. You should have heard these old time players scream over a simple 25 cent bet mistake. This type of pressure and the enormity of bets made me a better dealer. As time went by, I really understood the game.

My base salary was $27.50 per day. I would get a check every two weeks for $275. This is where the

W-2 comes in. The pay would be deducted for taxes. Tips I got on the other hand was a different story. Each night, when you showed up for work, you would get a small paper envelope. Inside the envelope was cash from the tips. It was great! There were no taxes paid out and there was no paper trail. All of the tips from the previous night were split up between all of the dealers which included the 21 dealers, roulette dealers and so on. Everybody always had ready cash on them. The money never hit your bank account. It was in your pocket. This is a high cash flow business. I normally made $17.50 a day in tips. So, if I include my normal pay, I was making about $225 a week which was not bad pay for the time.

For some reason, which I would soon find out, we always got paid in 50 cent increments. So, the tips would be $17.50, $18.50, $20.50 etc. We would normally never get an envelope with even money say $18. Each night, when I would show up and wait for the "call list" to be used, I would pick up my envelope with the tips. One night as I picked up my envelope and walked away, this old time dealer named Joe approached me. He told me: "Neal, every time you get an odd half buck in your base pay, you give it to Bill. That's his cigarette and drinking money. You go over $20 in tips, say like, $21.50, you give Bill $1.50. Do you understand?" I said I understood. The next night I stood and watched the other dealers collect their tip money. Sure enough, everybody was giving Scheduler Bill part of their tips. I learned a real valuable lesson. In order to get steady work, you need to pay the Scheduler, plain and simple. Also, I learned another lesson in the casino industry. Money talks!

The next night when I collected my Tokes, I gave Scheduler Bill two nights worth of odd change. He thanked me. Every night going forward I always gave Bill his piece of the Tokes. And guess what started to happen? I started to get more and more steady work from Bill. He would look at the list, act like he was reading it, look up and call out my name with more frequency. Then one day he called me and told me: "Liosi, you are assigned a permanent crew". It was great news. I did not have to worry about day to day work off the "call list". I was getting steady work. Of course, the next day, I gave Bill a little extra. It was my way of thanking him. He was a happy guy and so was I. Plus, I learned how things really worked in Vegas.

I was getting better at the crap game. To really learn the game, it takes about two years. Here I was eight months in and I had the game down cold. One night, there were sixteen people on the game. We had to have two Boxmen to watch it. In addition, there were two floor bosses watching and the eye in the sky or at that time, the telescope in the sky. They actually had guys in the ceiling using telescopes to watch the game. You could see them. The scopes they used were about two inches in diameter and you could see the scopes folding in and out in length. It was kind of funny.

I was on the pole and the prop bets were coming in fast and furious. I nailed them all and paid all of them out properly. I could see the bosses watching me and talking. Then they went over and pulled out a calculator. Calculators were brand new at the time and the casinos had to have them. They punched in some numbers, looked at each other, shook their heads up and down in agreement, and looked at me. I knew I paid it out correctly and they were gaining respect for me. Plus, the Boxmen started to pay significant attention to me. They could see I caught on.

This one Boxman took particular notice of me. We called him Winslow Drew. Why? He came to Vegas from Winslow, Arizona. He came to Vegas in 1966. He was downtown paying his dues because he got busted for stealing at the Stardust. He was lucky he did not get caught over at the Horseshoe. Benny Binion was an old time casino owner. He was tough and well respected. The word was if you got caught stealing at his place, he gave you two options. One was you would get reported to the police. The other was you would get your butt kicked by security. If you selected the last option, guess what, you took it like a man. He would then fire you. But, he would not put a word out on you. So the next day you could get a job next door.

Winslow Drew was on the twenty five cent game with me one night. It was my break time so I was walking over to the food counter and he grabbed me. "Kid, take a walk with me out to the car" he said. I did. No sooner did we get in his car, he pulled out a joint from under the seat and lit it up. I never smoked cigarettes or pot at the time. I couldn't believe he was smoking pot on our break. He asked me if I wanted a hit and I told him no. Then he asked me something which really caught me blindsided. Afterall, I looked up to these guys and wanted to get their job someday.

"Neal, would you be interested in stealing?" I was thinking to myself I can't believe what he just asked. Did this guy, who watches my payouts at the table, just ask me to steal? He sure the heck did! He told me he has a guy he works with. He told me he is called the "Agent". He then went into how they do it. "All you have to do is hand off five to ten red chips to him at a time periodically when there is a passing number. Don't pass off any greens or blacks. Do this for about ten to fifteen minutes. Just pass the chips to him. Okay?" He explained the bosses can't watch everything so they focus on the greens and blacks.

I asked Winslow: "How would I know who the Agent is?" He told me he is very tall, about six foot two, and very thin. He told me he is already in the casino and he will position himself next to you. I said okay and I left his car. Meanwhile he was still puffing on that joint when I was walking away.

Sure enough, within no time at all the Agent was standing right next to me at second base. Winslow got back from break and glanced my way. The Agent threw in twenty dollars for chips. I pushed it over to Winslow who changed it. The Agent made a pass line bet so not to attract attention. Back then, everybody is a pass line or right side bettor. A don't pass bettor was a rare breed. I couldn't believe what I was about to do. The shooter threw the dice and made his point. As I was making the payouts, I dropped off five reds in front of the agent. He picked them up off the table and placed them in the rack. It was that simple. It seemed so easy to me. There was a lot of action and confusion at the table. During this, I would continue to place stacks in front of the Agent. He stayed there for about 30 minutes and then he left.

The first night we grossed $225. We split it up three ways so I got $75. Lesson learned. I was making about fifty bucks from the Nugget. So, posting this guy I was able to more than double my pay overnight. What about the "eye in the sky"? Well, back then, it was not as sophisticated as it is today. There is only so much you can spot using the telescopes and binoculars. When you pass chips, it is hard to catch from upstairs. The Boxman is supposed to be looking out for this move. Since Winslow Drew was the Boxman, and he was running the scam, there was little chance of us getting caught.

We did this move three nights in a row. We made about $225 each night. On the third night, Winslow never paid me my share. I learned a valuable lesson! Never trust anyone! The next time I met Winslow in the hallway, I told him I was out. I never stole from the Nugget again.

I Finally Got on the Strip at the Flamingo.

Three

Flamingo - The Hustle

During this time period, all the dealers were white males. You never saw a woman working as a dealer. It was rare to see a black dealer. We had one black guy dealing craps and his name was "Earl the Pearl". He was an excellent dealer. There was an effort underway on the strip to integrate the dealers. Two bosses from the Sands came downtown and watched Earl deal for about a half hour. They immediately offered him a job at the Sands. He took it.

Getting a job on the Strip, especially at the Sands or Caesars, was like striking gold. It was the best blue collar job in America. I knew, I had to figure out a way to work there. So, I asked my brother for some help. He worked at the Stardust and had a lot of contacts. This was the Vegas way. You need to have contacts and connections to make it. Paulie told me he would make a call to Hymie Two Bags. What a name! Paulie and Hymie were good friends. Hymie was kind of a short guy who was very friendly to everyone. He also seemed to know everyone as well. Turns out he was a heavy with the mob. He was their "bagman" over at the Stardust. That's why we all called him Two Bags. He used two bags whenever he entered the count room. The next day, I got a call from the Flamingo to audition at 10 am. Pretty fast wasn't it. It was June of 1971. I showed up at 9:30 sharp.

The Bosses on the strip were somewhat sentimental for the dealers who broke in downtown. So, they did not give you a hard time right away. They knew you would be nervous and scared. They would start you out on a small game to see how you dealt and see if you had a good feel for the table. After dealing the 25 cents game at the Nugget, I really knew what I was doing. Within 15 minutes, they came over to me and moved me to a bigger game. I was on the higher end table for about fifteen minutes and one of the bosses came over and asked me: "When can you start?" I said:"Right away". They told me they would call me. This is how it worked. There were no applications to fill out, no hair clippings for drug tests, no background checks, and no paperwork with the exception of the W-2. These guys were the HR department. They did the hiring and they did the firing and they didn't get it approved by anyone and no one questioned them.

When I showed up for the first day on the job, I did my job perfectly. I settled in and they liked me. I gained their trust as a good dealer and that was one less thing they had to worry about. And there was one huge advantage working at the Flamingo. Tips were shared by the crew! Meaning, whatever amount of tips you made, you shared with the other three dealers you worked with on the shift. This was a big deal. The Nugget required you to split your tips with the entire shift. So, you would split tips with like 75 other dealers. Well, who is going to knock themselves out getting tips when it gets split 75 ways? Nobody!

The Flamingo was a different deal. You split the tips you made all night with three other dealers. If you get 400 dollars in tips at your table, you split it up at the end of the night and you walk away with a hundred. So, we were highly motivated as a crew to get as many tokes as possible. So we started "Hustling"!

"Hustling" is when you get a customer to tip you outright or have them make a bet for the dealers. It didn't take long for me to learn how to do it.

There are a lot of different methods to "Hustling". But before I get in to the methods, you have to understand, the Bosses and the Casino do not want you to get tips. That's right. They hated to see you get tips! Why? They see it as their money. Meaning, they figure a player will walk in the casino with a certain bankroll, say $500. Now, the casino wants the entire $500 in the fill boxes. Well, if the player starts tipping and placing bets for the dealers, the bosses see that as money leaving their pockets and getting shifted to the dealer's pockets. So, they despised it when a player tipped or made bets for the dealers. Hence, they created the "No Hustling Rule". If you got caught "Hustling players", meaning encouraging them to tip or bet for the crew, you got fired on the spot. Even if they suspected you doing it, they would fire you. Now, remember, there is no HR Department or Union to go to. They didn't exist. You had no one to appeal to. You would simply get fired.

There were a lot of different methods we would use to get tips for bets. But the very first thing you have to do is to let the Boxman know he is going to get "pieced off ", so he looks the other way! The Boxman knows pretty much everything going on at the table. That's why they are there. There is no question, he would hear us talking to the customers and there is no question he would see us using our methods. So, we had to let him know we would give him a piece of our tip action. In fact, it became an expectation.

You could make some good money hustling, so it was really worth the risk in doing it. Don't forget, the Floor Bosses would fire you in a second if they saw you do it. They would even creep up behind you and listen to what you said to the players. So, you had to be sharp and well aware of where everyone was. You really had to be aware of your surroundings. There was a real art in performing the "Hustle".

The first key method of getting tips and bets was to identify the customer who would be willing to part with their money if they see it benefiting them. You need a customer who is generally happy for the most part and it is even better if they are slightly intoxicated. You don't want him to be familiar with the dealers.

And you don't really want a regular. Sure, many of the regulars would give us bets, but they knew the routine and they normally would stick to it. The new customer on the other hand, who is there for the weekend to have a good time, he was a "mark". He or she is the guy we would zero in on. They were going to be our big score for the night. Our code name for these types of players was "George" or "Georgette". I have no idea who came up with this term. But that is how we would refer to them. If the mark was a really big tipper we would call him "King George".

The first rule working with a "George" is to be nice to him or her and give him some personality. Like, if the table is hitting the numbers, you would give him complements like he knew what he was doing. Just simple comments like "nice bet" and "dice are rolling your way". You would make some small talk to get him to like you. Then don't forget to help him with his betting! For example, if he forgot to place odds behind the pass line bet, I would give him a gentle reminder. "Mr. C. don't forget your odds bet." The odds bet behind the pass line is the best bet there is for a right player next to the come out roll. Or if he did a place bet on the four or the ten, I would ask him if he wanted to buy the number. This means he would pay five percent to buy the number and he would get paid the correct odds when he hits the point. If he put a bet on the Big Six or Big Eight located on the corner of the layout, I would remind him the Place Bet for Six and Eight is a better payout. Little reminders and small talk would get the players to warm up to the dealer. Eventually, he would identify with us as his friend and looking out for him.

Now, in order to get a George to make a bet for the dealers, you have to wait for the right moment. For starters, the Floor Boss and Shift Boss need to be busy doing something else. Secondly, and you get a feel for this, the dice have to be passing. Meaning the shooter is making numbers and winning. There is no sense asking for a bet when the table is ice cold. Not only will the dealer bet be a loser, "George" would be unhappy as well.

The numbers have to be hitting and then, when the time was right, I would just lean over softly and say "Mr. C. would you like to make a bet for the dealers? It makes for good luck." I'm telling you, ninety five percent of the time the "George" would make the bet. It was slick move. And when the table was running hot, George would be all too happy to make those bets. He would actually believe it was bringing him luck.

I also had some other hustling tricks. A real good confidence builder is to every so often pay George more money than he deserves. What? Yes, give him a higher payout. Say he had $5 on the pass line. If he hit, I would pay him ten bucks. At first he will be totally confused. He knew he was only supposed to get $5. It was funny to watch them. You know they would immediately pick up the chips and place them in the rack. Then, they would have a confused look on their face. Then the light bulb would go off and they realize you paid them extra on purpose. Now you have the guy hooked. By doing this trick, George immediately wants to thank you in some way and pay you back. What better way than direct tips or making a bet for the dealers? It worked every time.

And I like this one as well. Say, George had some place bets out there on the layout and it is time for the come out roll. The place bets are normally off play during the come out roll. That means you still leave the bets on the felt but there is no action on them. Now, there is an exception. The player can ask to have them in play. So, every so often, if one of

George's place bets hits on a come out roll, I would pay him and say out loud: "Mr. C., your bets were active on the come out, yes?" He was no dummy and would shake his head yes. He knew he got a free payoff and he would not forget the kindness.

Another tactic is to sincerely thank the George. Say, he makes a bet for the dealers, the shooter hits his point and the bet George made for the dealers wins. We would give him a big "Thank you so much Mr.C". It had to be heartfelt and if you knew his name you would address him respectfully. You can be sure you will get another bet from him. Probably a hardway or prop bet which is a great tip bet because they carry good payout odds. Or at least he would throw us a toke. It never fails and works every time. I learned early, giving recognition often creates repetition. It is like the Pavlov dog scenario.

In "Hustling" for tips, the customers just needed a little help. Once they caught on, it became natural for them to make a bet for the dealers or throw a toke in. Make no mistake about it, you had to hustle them. For example, let's say George makes a pass line bet for the dealers and the point four comes out. What you do is kindly ask him for the odds bet as well! They normally will do it if the table is hot. Now if the number hits, you get paid for the pass line and the odds on the odds bet. A ten dollar pass line bet combined with a ten dollar odds bet for a four point can net you a total of fifty bucks. That's a pretty good tip. I would never do it downtown because you would split your tips with the entire shift. Here at the Flamingo, you split tips with the other three guys on the crew. I could really relate to splitting it only four ways. And don't forget it was all cash and tax free! Well, we still had to piece off the Boxman and don't forget the scheduler. The scheduler kept our crew together. It was just the cost of doing business.

The other guys on the crew were hustling just as hard as me. We would look down the table at each other and nod to identify the Georges at the table. As for the dealer who might be on break, when he returned to take over the stick, I would thank the George directly for the bets and tap the stick a few times in his direction. I would do it in such a fashion so the whole table of customers could see how you are treated when you make bets and tips for the dealers. Other players would want that type of recognition as well. So, they were encouraged to tip so they could be stars of the table. Another plus is people always appreciate getting a nice respectful "Thank You" from the dealers. It makes them feel important and appreciated. Plus the added benefit is the dealer coming off break would know who the Georges were. Then they could start working on them. It was great. Every guy on the crew was in tune and the Boxman was looking the other way.

Now if you give this some thought, you could make some pretty good money quickly by hustling. Let's say you are working an eight hour shift and you get one tip or bet per hour. You are talking about $20 to $50 an hour in tips. Times that amount by eight hours, times four dealers, and you will see the money adds up quickly. Some nights when the dice are passing, say on a Friday or Saturday night, the money just poured over our way. We could make $200 a night in tips each. That's about $1200 in today's buying power. This was a high cash business and we had the cash. We were carrying around three to five hundred with us all of the time. In most parts of the country, it was rare to see someone pull out a hundred dollar bill. Not in this business. There was cash flowing everywhere. Hustling paid off nicely!

But as I said earlier, you had to be extremely careful when hustling. If a Boss caught you, you would be history and just that fast. These guys acted like the money was coming out of their own pocket. You didn't have to worry about the Boxman since you were piecing him off. The Bosses would sometimes take paybacks as well. We would give some perks like a new suit, or a carton of cigarettes, stuff like that. It kept it peaceful with them.

Some of these guys like Jockey Rose would be fanatical and crazy when the table was playing in the customer's favor. Between our hustling and a table getting smoking hot, Jockey would go nuts seeing a table lose money. One time, there was a table which was red hot. The shooter was making passes for at least 30 minutes. Jockey would start pacing back and forth in the pit area. You could see the smoke coming off of him. Then he would come over and slow the game down by picking up and inspecting the dice. Of course, everyone on the table would scream at him, but he didn't care. I think he liked screwing around with people. He was that fanatical.

I remember another time, the table was red hot. Jockey walked up behind the stick man and told him:

"If you don't have the shooter seven out on the next throw, I am going to fire you." Sure enough, the shooter threw an **eight**. The stickman said out loud: **"Seven out!"** even though the point was an eight! Jockey fired him anyway! That's how worked up these pit bosses would go.

We had this one table which always seemed to be a loser for the casino. Jockey would stand there and watch and watch and watch, trying to figure out how this table could not make any money. It got to the point where he brought in some experts, former cheats themselves, to see how this table lost. After a few nights, they told Jockey there was nothing wrong with the game. They assured him the odds have to change eventually in favor of the casino. He didn't know what to do. He would just keep pacing behind it.

It was late one night around 1 A.M. I was on the pole at the Hard Luck Table. I called it the Hard Luck Table since it had no luck for the casino. This night, the pass line players were making a bundle. I couldn't remember the last time we saw a craps thrown or a seven out. Suddenly, Jockey came over and said: "We're shutting this game down." The players were screaming at him but he didn't care. He replied to them: "It's my game and I can close the damn thing down anytime I want." He told the craps crew to close it up and open a new game at another table. We did what he told us to do. About an hour later, there he was standing there staring at the Hard Luck Table. About an hour passed and he shows up with six guys from the porter crew. Jockey was given them directions. Next, they picked up the table and took it off the casino floor. The last I heard is they brought it out to Carson Street and took several axes to it. That was the end of the Hard Luck Table. This is how fanatical these guys were.

At this time, I started to make some serious money. I was on the strip and I was working with a crew. The cash was coming in. But for me it didn't seem to be enough. I was making about $150 to $250 a shift. I needed to make more money. I thought about my stretch downtown with Winslow Drew. It finally hit me!

Four

THE AGENT

I thought about my time with Winslow Drew. He and I were making a few hundred dollars a night stealing off the table. I was thinking about how I could run my own game at stealing. Winslow taught me how to do it. But I needed to find an Agent. I normally went to the gym three to four times a week. There was this guy I would talk to once in a while. As time went on, I started to have longer conversations with him. His name was Uncle Dennis. He was a manager of a facility which was a gas station and food market. I had a feeling he wasn't making much money on that job. So, one day I asked him if he would be interested in making some additional cash. Of course, he said.

I told him the scam is simple. I would call him when the casino was busy and the tables were packed. When this much action is going on, no one can keep an eye on everything including the eye in the sky. Speaking of the eye in the sky, the casinos were just putting in cameras. So, above every table there was a two way mirror glass. The glass dimensions were about two feet by two feet. But get this, if you stood at just the right angle, you could see the camera on its rotating dial. You could actually see where the camera was looking! Can you believe it? So, we knew where the camera was looking. All the while the casino was getting more confident thinking their new surveillance technology was improving their watch on us. Little did they know we could see the camera and where it was pointing.

We had a good crew working together, hustling and making some big bucks. We decided to work the night shift and work the bigger games. Those were the games with higher minimum wagers and you would see mostly greens and blacks on the table. I spoke to Uncle Dennis at the gym and explained to him how simple the move is. I would call him on my break and tell him to come over. Since he was the food market/gas station manager, he could come and go as he wished. It usually took him no more than ten minutes to be in place. The gas station was next to Caesars. All he had to do was change his shirt and walk across the street.

I always operated the scam from 2nd base. For one reason, I could see the camera. Reason number two, I was right handed so it was easier to do the hand off. And since the Boxman is to the left of me he has an obstructed view. Plus, I knew how to make the view more obstructed. I was good enough where I could do pay outs with both hands at the same time. Of course, the casino didn't like it. The casino has a very specific method of paying customers. It had to be in order. You pay the customer straight in front of you first and then you go player by player working left to right. With some bets, like the field and place bets, you pay the players who make the wagers. So, I developed this technique where I would have whites (one dollar chips) on the left side of me and the right side of me. So the chip line going left to right would be whites, blacks, greens, reds, and whites. Using the two handed payout method just created more confusion on the table and made it harder to track the action. That's if the Boxman really cared. Most of these guys were screw ups and only cared about getting tips from us. We would call some of these guys "sleepers" because they would try to sit there and act like they were watching. I remember this one old guy who would actually fall asleep once in a while!

The next part of the scam requires the dice to be traveling away from second base to the other side of the table. So it is best when the shooter is down by my side. Once the shooter throws the dice, the stickman watches the dice leave the shooter's hand and delays one second to make sure he only has two dice in his hand. Then, everyone on the table, including the stickman, watches the dice roll down the far side of the felt. **This is when you do the pass!**

I kept hearing Winslow Drew in my head saying: "just pass the stack over to the Agent". I taught Uncle Dennis well. He just needed to keep his eyes open and at the right time, I would pass red chips over his way. I told him: "You just pick them up and put them in the rail. It's that simple". I wanted him to keep the chips in the rail so I could count them. I didn't want him to rip me off. I learned this the hard way when Winslow Drew ripped me off at the Nugget.

One night, the situation was right. The casino floor was crowded. The crap tables were packed and there was plenty of money on the felt. Now was the time! I called Uncle Dennis. He was there in ten minutes and he made his way next to me. He would buy in for $100. Everything was working as planned to this point. All the elements of the scam were in place. The shooter was on our side of the table and he threw the dice. I quickly handed off five red chips to Uncle Dennis. He reached down, picked them up and placed them on the rail. It worked without a hitch. I did the hand off twice in about twenty minutes. Each time I pushed five red chips over to him for a total of fifty dollars. I did not want to push it. Plus, I wanted to see how Uncle Dennis would handle himself. He was perfect. After the second hand off, I nodded to him and he left and walked to the cage to cash in.

After my shift, I went to the station to meet him. I told him we had a good first go at it and we were to split it fifty/fifty, this time. I told him there would be bigger payouts in the future. However, going forward, he would get a 25% split. Why? I told him the Boxman and the Floor Boss both needed to get 25% of their end of the action for looking the other way. So, the next time, he would keep 25% and I would get 75%. I would keep 25% for myself the other 50% to piece off the other partners. Well guess what? He fell for it. There was nobody else involved! It was just him and me. So, I kept the remaining 75% for myself. It was some scam. Not only did I scam the casino, I was scamming the participant in the scam! I figured I was taking the most risks so I should get most of the money. I also told him we are going to raise the stakes. I was going to pass more chips to him more often at the next visit.

The following night we tried it again. This time he would stay at the table for a few cycles of the dealers. The dealers work a position for twenty minutes and move to the next position or go to break. Once my twenty minutes were up, I would go to break. When I returned I would relieve the stickman who trades places with the 3rd base. So, I would not get back to 2nd base to work the scam for sixty minutes. Uncle Dennis would either take a break himself or wait for me to return from break which means he would reduce his bet to the minimum. Now, the key to pulling all of this off is to strike fast and do it in a short period of time. The other eight hours of the shift you would focus on hustling. If you make your moves fast and in a short period of time, it is going to be really hard to get caught.

When The Dealers Robbed Vegas....And Other Tales

The next move I made with Uncle Dennis was worth $200. It was a similar busy night. We made this score in about 15 minutes. I did four handoffs to him. He kept $50 and I got $150. Pretty good move wouldn't you say? Do you think I would stop there? No way!

I had my own methods to get chips in my pocket. During the 1970s the dealers actually had pockets on their shirts. Some poker houses still employ this technique but it is rare to see. Why did we have pockets? The dealer working the stick had no place to put tips or dealer bets when they happened. So he would place them in his shirt pocket. We never stole any chips when we were working the pole. There were just too many eyes looking at you. You controlled the game and everyone at the table was watching you. They were watching how you handled the dice with the stick and where you were moving the dice on the table. The shooter normally had his eyes glued to you and the dice. So, there was no way you could risk stealing any chips. There was a side benefit to this. Everybody is watching the dice and the stickman. So, who is watching the dealers at 2nd and 3rd base? Not a lot of eyes! So, we were able to do our thing pretty easily. One thing was for sure though. When the stickman got tapped off the pole to move, you better believe all the dealers watched him like hawks and made sure the tips in his upper pocket found their way to the tip box. You cheat the casino but you better not cheat us the dealers.

I used this method a lot. I also used another terrific move. I called this the "Move of the Century". You need a big game with a lot of action, a lot of players and a lot of greens and blacks on the table. You had to keep your eye on the camera to make sure it was pointed down table, keep an eye on the floor to make sure they were busy and the Boxman was busy as well. Now, keep in mind you have 8 hours to wait and pick your points to pull these moves. So, you just have to be patient and wait for the right time.

The next thing is you wait for a seven out. At this point, you have to clean the table of chips and place them in the columns in front of you. Everyone wants you to hurry so to get the action back going again. I was practicing this move at home for weeks before I tried it out live. What I did next was clean the table after the seven out and place the chips in columns in front of me by color. I trained myself to be able

When The Dealers Robbed Vegas....And Other Tales

to pull my hand away from a column I was arranging and keep one to three chips in my palm. It was like second nature to me since I have been practicing at home for the past few weeks. Then the only last step was to get the money in my pocket. It was simple. When no one was looking, I would slip my index finger in my right side pocket and drop the chips. With one move, I could drop 2 or 3 greens or a black or two. I was slick doing it. Remember, you only need to make this move a few times a night to make $100 to $200 a night. It was all about timing and the move as slick as possible.

Cleaning the table was not the only opportunity you got to pull this move. You can do it when you paid out as well. I would cup a stack of chips and pay the players when they won on the pass line. When I was done, I would still have a chip or two in my hand. No one could tell I had something in my hand. At the right time, I would do the drop into the old pocket.

Do you think I was the only dealer doing this? No way! Everybody was scoring with one method or another. We had this one dealer who actually came to work wearing panty hose! He would cup the chips, act like he was adjusting his belt, and bam, drop the chips into the panty hose. And then there was this other dealer who actually lined aluminum foil inside his underpants thinking the chips would be caught in his aluminum pants and not slide out down by his leg. I do not know why he didn't wear panty hose like the other guy. The panty hose method was pretty good. Me? I just put them in my pant pockets.

And get this, even the dealers were stealing chips from the other dealers. Can you believe it? In many of the Casinos, all the dealers would share equally in the tokes. So the craps dealers would pool their tips together and split them based on the number of craps dealers on their shift. The 21 dealers would do the same and only split them with the 21 dealers. It was the "Toke Committee's" job to collect and count the tokes before going to the cage. Towards the end of the shift, there were normally two to three dealers who would go from table to table saying hello and picking up the tip boxes and replacing them with empty ones. They would put them on a cart and wheel to the next table. Once, they finished their collection they would go upstairs to count them. There, they would empty all of the boxes and organize them by color on racks. Last stop was delivery to the cage. Once at the cage, the girls would count the chips, total the cash, and fill out a slip showing the take for the shift and the number of dealers working. The cage then knew what to pay each dealer in tips the next day in their little envelope. This was the process.

So, how do dealers get a chance to steal from the other dealers? Get on the Toke Committee! How do you get on the Toke Committee? You are voted in by the other dealers. Yeah, every six months a vote for the Toke committee would be held.

Why did the Casinos have the dealers share the tips with the entire shift? Dealers are less motivated to hustle for tips when it gets split up with so many other dealers. Why take a risk hustling a five dollar bet when it gets split 75 ways? As a dealer, you wouldn't risk your job hustling with such a small reward. Now remember, the Casino doesn't want you to get tips! It was less money for them. They hated to see any dealer get a tip.

Anyway, these guys Vinnie, Sal and James would get voted in every six months at the Flamingo. We would see them at the end of every shift coming by, saying hello and picking up the boxes. These guys just seemed to always get elected. One time, believe it or not, they actually lost the election. We had new members to the Toke Committee. So, what do you think happened next? The tip payout to the dealers went up $20 per dealer per day. Can you believe this? These guys were stealing about $100 each time they came down after making the count. They made their move transporting the chips to the cage after the count. Of course, we couldn't prove it, but explain how the tip drop went up and stayed up. It also turns out they were rigging the elections every six months and the one time they refused to pay the person who counted the ballots. So, they lost the election. What a scam! It worked for years.

Even the Security team was stealing and taking tips to look the other way. Get a load of what Security was doing down at the Fremont. Security was in charge of making the pickups of cash boxes from the tables. Usually, there were two Security Guards detailed to this job. As they stop at each table, the Boxman and the Floor Boss would tally up the chips left on the table, fill out a "fill slip" with the amount of chips left on the table, and place the fill slip in the cash box which is locked. Now, the Guards had the keys to the cash boxes. Imagine that! After the Guards would collect all of the boxes, they would march them to the count room.

When The Dealers Robbed Vegas....And Other Tales

At the Fremont, the count room was on an upper floor. This made it harder for someone to rob the Casino. So, the Guards would use the elevator to get the cash boxes to the count room. This was the normal procedure. One day when they arrived at the count room, two boxes were missing 'fill slips'. How was this possible? You know the floor was filling out the slips and placing them in the locked cash box. Where could the slips be? Well, if they checked the pockets of the guards, not only would they have found the fill slips, they would also find a pocket full of cash. What happened is, the guards in their haste, opened up the boxes and grab hands full of cash while they were transporting them in the elevator. Only this time, they accidentally grabbed the fill slips along with the cash. The gig was up. The casino placed cameras in the elevator so to watch them while they were in there. Turns out they had this scam going on for years. It was amazing how they would be able to get a few boxes opened, grab the cash, and close it all back up within a few seconds it took for the elevator to go up. The Casino had no idea and never saw this one coming.

Don't think the folks in the count room were angels. They were stealing as well. With all of that cash in front of you, who could resist? At the Flamingo, they had three guys working the count room and one gal watching them. Each morning like clockwork around 4 am, here she comes out of the count room walking across the casino floor on the way to the café. She was dispatched to get some coffee and sodas for the crew back in the count room. And while she was away, who was watching the guys in the room? Nobody! They were going to town taking money. She would take no more than ten minutes to go to the café and return with coffee. It was plenty of time for the guys in the count room to do their thing. Of course, the guys in the room would piece her off. So, she kept her mouth shut. She knew a good thing when she saw it.

The Bid Daddy of them all was Hymie Two Bags. Remember him? He was the guy my brother called to get me the job at the Flamingo. He would come in the casino about twice a month. He always looked good in a suit. What you see in the movies is the mob guy who slyly walks in with a briefcase and ducks in the count room. While I am sure it was this way in some casinos, at the Flamingo it was Hymie who showed up with two bags. Only, he knew everybody. I mean everybody. Floor bosses, Shift Bosses, Dealers, Boxman, Bartenders, Cocktail Waitresses, and even the Players! He would go around and say hello to everyone. Sometimes he would stay for a drink or have dinner over at the steakhouse. After he was done he would simply walk over to the cage and next thing you know you see him walking out the door. No one questioned a thing. We did not even talk about it between ourselves. How the place stayed in business with all of us stealing is a testament to how much money these Casinos were making.

Things were going good for me. Uncle Dennis was working out well and I started to hand off some blacks to him on a regular basis. Once he had the chips, he had to turn them into cash. Things were a bit looser then and he would just walk up to the cage and cash in about $300 to $500 a visit. He would normally have no problem. I told him to make sure to give the girl at the cage a nice tip like $10 and every so often give her $25. So, what did she care how many chips you were cashing. She was getting her tip. This is the move you need to make. You have to tip everyone along the way. It didn't matter to me since it kept things going and we were raking it in. It would be much harder to do it today. If someone walks up to the cage with $10,000 in chips, you can be sure the eye in the sky and the pit would get a call.

So, you have to be smart about cashing in the chips. One New Years Eve, we walked off with $4,000. It took us two weeks to exchange the chips without raising suspicions.

The chips I took home was a different story. When I came home, my wife was normally asleep. Oh yeah, I forgot to mention. Along the way I got married to wife #2. She was great. Later on I would really screw this up but for right now we were doing great. A few years back while working at the Nugget, I called her out of the blue on a Sunday night. I wasn't picked off the call list this particular night. I asked her to get married right over the phone and she said yes. I called my brother and asked him and his wife to stand in as witnesses. He threw a fit and yelled at me and told me there was no way he was going down there on his night off. The next thing I knew, my wife to be and I were at the "Little Church of the West". They had some people that hanged out there who would step in as witnesses. So, we got married just that fast. It all happened in just a few hours, Vegas style.

Anyway, I would come home from work and empty my pockets and stack chips on the table of every color. She would see them the next morning before she went to work as an x-ray technician at the hospital. After a while, and as the stacks were getting higher, she suspected something and finally asked me where all the chips were coming from. I was honest with her and told her every dealer was doing it. I told her it was like part of the job. Now the problem is, I had the chips stacking up and I needed a way to cash them. I couldn't do it since we were not allowed to gamble at the casino. It would be a real tip off if I showed up at the cage with chips. So, I asked her if she would help me out. I told her: "All you have to do is walk up, pass the chips to the person at the cage and return with the cash. Make sure no one is following you because you are returning to me at the car." She said she would give it a try.

So, we went to the Casino about two hours before my shift started. I gave her $500 in chips and told her to make sure no one was following. She returned a huge mess. I thought she was having a nervous breakdown. She was terrified. But she did return with the cash. I knew she would be no good going forward. She was too honest and didn't have it in her. Like I said before, it needs to be in your DNA. Not everyone can do it. There is too much pressure worrying about being caught. So, now I had a problem. I had about

$5000 in chips I needed to cash and no way to get it done. An idea popped in my head. Uncle Dennis! He was fearless. He had the low paying job down at the station so he needed money. He was doing great as the Agent. So, I made a deal with him. He would get to keep 20% of the cash from the chips I gave him to cash out. Of course he said yes! So, I put that part of the puzzle in place. It worked out perfectly.

The guys robbing the slot machines with the tools had a similar problem. How do you cash in all those tokens without raising any suspicion? Back in those days, you played the slot machines with tokens, like slugs. Each casino had their own type. Once you were ready to cash out, you get a plastic bucket and fill it with tokens. Then you would walk to a slot machine redemption area. They were throughout the casino floor. They often were inside of a circular bank of slot machines and they were elevated. So, you hand up the bucket to them, they would put it though the token machine and pay you off. How do you not raise suspicion when you walk up with say $500 in tokens? Simple, ask the Suzzie G. who's working the slot token redemption to give you $400. She got the idea quickly and you were up in running.

When The Dealers Robbed Vegas....And Other Tales

Things were going good. I was collecting a salary, hustling for tips and bets, passing off chips to my Agent, and stealing on my own. The cash was pouring in. How much did I steal at this point? I really don't know. What I do know is this: I was 24 years old. I bought a 1971 Corvette off this guy and paid him $4900 in cash. I bought a Witchcraft Ski Boat for $4800 and I paid it in cash. I moved from East Charleston to Russell Road on the East side and I put down 20% in cash. The area between Russell Road and Sahara on the East side of town was the happening area. You could get a half acre in a property which was rare in Vegas. The house I bought was gorgeous. The best places to eat and party were located between Russell and Sahara. We were living good. I put a $10,000 pool in the back yard and I paid for it in cash. I had $25,000 in cash in a safety deposit box at the local bank which has the buying power of $150,000 today! All this and I was only 24 years old.

One day, I came home, walked in and told my wife I quit my job at the Flamingo. I knew the odds! Sooner or later I would get caught. And if they identified you as stealing, they didn't just walk down and fire you, although they would often do so. They would watch and follow you to see who you were working with, associating with, where you lived, and so forth. I knew I pushed the limit of my luck. So, I quit while I was ahead. The town needed dealers and I knew I could quickly get a job somewhere else.

Here is the Old MGM Grand – Now Ballys.

Five

MGM – The Crew

When MGM opened, it was the largest casino in the world. Kirk Kerkorian created it and he was a genius. He demolished the old Bonanza and built this terrific property right there on the Strip at Las Vegas Boulevard and Flamingo. It was across the street from the Barbary Coast (today the Cromwell) and the Dunes (today the Bellagio). This was the epicenter of the strip. Caesars was caddy corner away and was still the highest end Casino in town. My brother, Paulie, did his time downtown and he was back as a craps dealer in Caesars. I thought I was a great dealer but he was better.

Kerkorian said he was going to build a casino where no one needed to leave. He was right. Everything you wanted was right there in one place and one building. There were several restaurants of all types, nightclubs, two showrooms, a huge casino floor, the newest slot machines, and get this, he even put in a bowling alley, a movie theatre, and a shopping mall. He was ahead of his time. There was no reason to leave the place.

It was a very classy place. They even had a true Baccarat Pit. The Baccarat area was actually sunken down from the floor by about five feet. There was a railing around so people would not trip and fall in. It was a great attraction. People would come in just to see the action. It was one of the few strictly cash games. There were no chips, just stacks of cash. People would be amazed at the enormity of cash sitting on the tables. There were stacks and stacks of them. The dealers would soap up the money before they opened the table. When they paid out, they would snap the bills out and the bills would float down and lay in a fan for the players to collect. These guys were good. It was amazing just to stand there and watch them handle the cash and the cards. It was quite an attraction.

Now, can you imagine how much cash was stolen out of the Baccarat Pit. One of the dealers which I chose not to name, stole enough money out of there to open up one of the finest restaurants in town. I didn't work with those dealers but you just know they were robbing. After all, how do you think he got enough money to open up a restaurant in just a few years? How do you get such capital? You don't get it from a dealer's salary that's for sure!

The MGM was also one of the biggest craps games in town. There were ten tables going. You take the location of the hotel, all of the amenities the hotel offered, the first class entertainment, and a brilliant owner to boot, you just know the money is flowing. I had to get a job there.

Remember, there is no H.R. Department. You don't fill out an application. So, how do you get a job there? You have got to have JUICE! That's the way it worked in Vegas. You needed to know someone who knew someone who would put a good word in for you so you could get a job. Who did I know who could help me out? None other than Paulie!

Now, Paulie was making about 70 to 80 thousand dollars a year legitimately at Caesars. So, he was doing pretty good. He also seemed to know everybody. In fact, he used to have one of the shift bosses over for pasta dinner on Sundays. This shift boss was an Asian guy named Dave Yic. Yes, I know it is a strange name for an Asian guy. Anyway, Paulie asked Yic to call Chas Walsh at the MGM and asked him to put me to work. Shortly thereafter, Paulie called me and told me to see Chas Walsh. As soon as I saw him he said: "Your Paulie's little brother, right?" I said yes and he told me to see Ron Trip the scheduler. Before you know it I was back at work and on the swing shift.

Incidentally, the swing shift is the best shift to work on. The hours are normally 5 PM to 1 AM, 6 to 2, 7 to 3, or 8 to 4. These are the hours most people play the tables. The players normally had a nice dinner and saw a great show. There were two showrooms with two shows a night. The best entertainers in the world would come to perform. The casino would be packed. It was a great atmosphere and the money was flowing like crazy. I was placed on a crew by the scheduler and placed on the 8 PM to 4 AM shift.

When The Dealers Robbed Vegas....And Other Tales

Not only was it great to work at the MGM due to the money flowing, the other great thing was the tip action was crew for crew. The crew you worked with shared the tips with the other guys on the crew. So, if you get with a good crew who knows how to work and hustle the customers for tips, you are going to make a lot of money.

I was new, so you better believe I was doing a great job and watching myself. I didn't want to get fired especially since my brother got the job for me. I would do a little hustling but nothing much. I first needed to get the respect from the other dealers, the Boxman and the Floor Bosses. I needed to show them I knew how to deal. I was really good at it so, it didn't take long for them to see how good I really was. I was back and I was on my best behavior.

After about three months, I was on the stick during a game and I had my first introduction to this guy named Jackie Gums. He also was a friend of my brothers. He sat down, looked at me and said: "You are Paulie's brother aren't you?" You see the word travels fast in this industry. I said I was. He then said: "Dice Out" and I started dealing the game. Jackie Gums was a really sharp dresser and he also had a really sharp mind. He did not miss a thing on the green felt. He could spot a mispay a mile away. Nothing would get by him. But I thought two things were strange about him. First, he was called Jackie Gums because he had no teeth. I mean he had dentures but at the table he never wore them. Also, he was always eager to help the dealers clean up the chips. Jackie never missed a chance to help clean up. You won't see that today. Today, the dealers clean up and pass the stack to the Floor who tucks it away. The Boxmen were eventually replaced by Floor Supervisors. Of course, the rules back then were a little looser than today. So, it did not seem that unusual to see the Boxman help out.

Keep in mind, most dealers and boxmen had one type of issue or another. Most of them were degenerate gamblers themselves. In addition, a lot of the dealers started doing coke when it hit town. So, many of them had bad habits they need to feed. And if you know something about a bad habit, you can never feed it enough. It will always want more until there is a crisis. A lot of the dealers would come to work so high, I couldn't believe they could keep track of the game and often they didn't. Why didn't they get fired? They were juiced in. Somebody in the hierarchy owed somebody a favor, so they kept their job.

You know, there were people in town who had a lot of power back then. A lot of these guys were there to protect the skim. When these guys called, people jumped to attention. For example: I remember this one floor boss back at the Flamingo named Nate Glassman. He was a Jewish guy who would smoke these big fat cigars. For some reason, he didn't like me. He would often be verbally abusive and always call me "boy" very disrespectfully. One night, we had a junket come in from New York City with a bunch of Italian guys here to play for a few days. They were at my table. Two of these guys were next to me at second base. The table was on a roll and hitting a bunch of numbers. Whenever this happened, the Floor Bosses would try to upset the game by doing all kinds of goofy stuff. For example, they would do things, like stop the game and inspect the dice. Other actions included trying to change out the dice. Of course, the players hated these tactics. When the dice are running hot, no one wants anyone to screw up the flow of the game. If the Floor Boss tried to screw things up you would get players yelling and screaming at him. I mean, it would be crazy. I would hear every foul mouth word you could think of coming out of the mouths of these players. They knew what the Floor Boss was trying to do. He was trying to change the luck of the game. Sometimes the Floor Boss would respond to the players by saying: "Hey, this is our game and we will run it any way we want. And if you don't like it, you can play somewhere else."

On this particular occasion, these New York guys were obviously tired from their trip and were enjoying a good run on the dice. I was friendly to them like I am to all customers in order to get some tips. Meanwhile, Nate comes up to the table and starts being abusive to me calling me boy, do this, do that, you are no good, etc.. The two guys from New York look at him and one of them said in my defense: "Who do you think you are talking to?" Nate said he would talk to his employees anyway he likes. The next thing you know, these two guys from New York attack Nate and start beating him. They both jumped on him at the same time and started pounding Nate. I couldn't believe my eyes. Security quickly came over and broke it up. You would think they would call the cops or at least toss these two guys out the door. Nope! They wanted their money. So, they shrugged it off and everyone went right back to playing the game.

Meanwhile, Nate went to the men's room to clean himself up and settle down. I never saw such a thing.

The next day I get a call from my brother. He asked me: "Neal, what the heck happened over there last night? I'm getting calls from everybody." I told him exactly what took place. I told him how the fight got started by Nate calling me boy, etc. Paulie then said: "Okay. Let me review it with Hymie." I didn't think much more about it. I went to work as normal.

When I got there and started my shift, Nate came over to me. The way he acted, you would think I was Nate's long lost cousin. A total 100% change in the way he treated me. He kept checking on me, apologizing and seeing if I needed anything. I think if I asked him to pay my mortgage, he would have. Obviously, someone had a talk with him and it could only come from one place. You see, there were, and are, powerful people in this town and if you are juiced in, you are protected and you get favors. My brother had connections with most of the people in town. I am sure the report back to Hymie created a few phone calls. This is the way Vegas worked back then. Nate never talked disrespectfully towards me again the entire time I worked at the Flamingo.

At the MGM, I was really confused why Jackie Gums took his teeth out before sitting at the game up until one night. I was working the pole directly across from him. It was a normal busy night with some of the regular customers and a number of new players. I was controlling the game. I passed the dice to the shooter and he "Seven'd Out." We, the dealers, immediately started clearing the table. Jackie helped us clear the table so often, it seemed to be normal for him to do it. This time, I see Jackie clearing away chips and he slides a stack of blacks back to the rack. When he was doing this, he tilted his hand slightly to me and showed me three black chips cupped in his hand. He looked me directly in the eyes, smiled, moved his hand to his mouth and put the chips in his mouth in one smooth motion. I couldn't believe my eyes! I was stunned! He then motioned me to start a new game. No wonder why he never wore his teeth! This guy was stealing hundreds in his mouth and then taking them out during his break. In fact, I would realize later, he would only make the move when it was his turn to take a break. This way he didn't have to worry about talking and the chips didn't need to stay in his mouth so long. It was unbelievable. And what did I think about after I got over my shock? I thought to myself: "Hey, I might have a new partner!"

After Jackie Gums realized I was not going to rat him out and neither would the other dealers, he started to take us under his wing and teach us new angles. Of course, each new method and angle was to teach us how to steal money from the Casino and hustle tips. His goal of course was to get more tips to the dealers so we could piece him off later. But first he figured that he had to train us and make us work as a team.

At this time, we worked as a crew for six weeks. After the six weeks were up, the scheduler would switch the dealers around so you worked with a new crew. They didn't want you to get too close with the other dealers. The MGM was a new joint and they played it safe and by the book. It wasn't like Downtown where you could piece off the scheduler and stay on the same crew. The scheduler here was going to enforce the rules. So, you got about six weeks to steal as much as possible with the guys you trusted.

The guys I worked with on the first crew were all characters and they had plenty of experience. Tommy Socks came from some casino in the Bahamas, so he knew his way around. He was a big guy, over six foot and built. He worked out somewhere. He was a nice guy but all too greedy. In fact, he was so greedy, he had his wife become a pro boxer. Yep! He wanted to make a pay day out of her. She had absolutely no business getting in a ring. On her first fight at the Silver Slipper, she was beaten so bad, she was almost killed. Tommy would try to hustle a buck any way he could. And he was definitely good at hustling tips off of the customers.

Then there was this guy Eddie Earth Shoes. He was short and stocky and a barrel full of laughs. He always was positive and happy making other people laugh as well. Eddie and Tommy came up with this crazy idea which actually worked and earned them their names. Eddie had a small shoe store which his wife would run. He knew the dealers were always leaning over the table placing the bets, paying off and making change. It can be tough on your back after a few hours. They came up with an idea to switch the location of the heal on the shoes from the back to the front of the shoe. They had thousands of these shoes made and started selling them to the dealers. I even bought a pair. At first, the shoes were more comfortable when dealing. But after a few days, it was actually worse on your back. In two days, I had such a pain in my back I could barely walk. I wasn't alone. You could see dealers walking around with their hand on their back rubbing it. You got to hand it to Eddie and Tommy. They made a fortune off this scam. They sold thousands of shoes which all ended up being thrown away in the trash can. Everybody loved Eddie and Tommy so they didn't get mad at them, they just gave them the nicknames of Socks and Earth Shoes.

The third guy on our crew was Pete the Whistle. He was a normal looking guy and kind of quiet. He was pretty straight laced. He came in to work and kept his head down. He got his nickname later on. But for right now, we knew he would work with us.

One Friday night we were working as a crew and Jackie Gums was the Boxman. It was a really busy night. The place was packed and so were the tables. All ten tables were open. This is the perfect environment. There has to be organized chaos to pull off this next move. For one reason, the eye in the sky and the Floor can't keep an eye on everything. So, they focus on the winning tables. They don't care if people lose. The Players are suppose to lose. So their focus is on the winning tables to figure out if someone is cheating or just to screw up the flow of the game. A night like this would be a perfect night working with my

Agent, Uncle Dennis. But, I was still new to the hotel and didn't want to push my luck this early.

On a night with this much action, there are chips and bets being thrown in all of the time. A lot of people like to bet the prop bets due to the high payouts. This night was no different and there were plenty of prop bets. Often, the game moves so fast, I do not have the chance of properly arranging the chips in the prop boxes. I was a pro though. For me, it was easy to remember who made the bet and what amount. When the shooter tossed the dice, I would have enough time to organize the bets while the other dealers paid out the come bets, field bet and place bets.

This night Jackie Gums would press me to keep the dice in play. I did. On this one roll, the dice came out a twelve. So, as the stickman, I needed to pay off the patrons who made a one roll prop bet on the twelve. Now, the chips were a little disorganized on the prop bet area so it is difficult to tell who made the bet. Not for me. I knew it cold. I started to pay off the patrons and Jackie Gums looked at me and told me I forgot to pay off Mr. C (a customer) and reminded me Mr. C also had $5 in play for the dealers. I looked at him dead in the eyes and I immediately figured out what he was doing. This would be a big pay out for the dealers. The odds are 30 to 1 for a single roll twelve. That five dollar bet would become a hundred fifty dollar tip for the dealers. Doing this move never occurred to me. What a move! Mr. C did have money out on the prop bets but it was for a hard eight not a one roll twelve. Well, who knows except me and the Boxman. I simply moved his bet over to the c-e and paid off Mister C. I also thanked him for the bet he made for the dealers by tapping the stick in his direction and paid off the dealers by placing the $150 in my top pocket. This was a great move. We were going to make a lot of money doing this.

Later, I found out this move was called a "Phantom Bet" and also known as "Past Posting". "Past Posting" is when you place a bet on a number after the outcome is known. In this case, the twelve came out. We knew the outcome so now you just place a bet on the outcome which was meant for another number. Mr. C didn't care. He just got a nice payout. The "Phantom Bet" is when you say there was a bet on a number but there never was. There was no real bet. You as the stickman just say there is a bet and pay off accordingly. In this case, the Dealers were paid off.

With so much chaos and the chips scattered about in front of me during this game, no one could track what happened. You normally rely on the Stick Man to properly keep track of the bets and you rely on the Boxman to make corrections to any mistakes made by the Dealers. Well, with Jackie as a partner and actually teaching us the tricks, you only had to worry about the eye in the sky and the Floor Boss. Since, you are working the Pole Position, you can see where everyone is. It is all about timing and not being too greedy. After I made the payoff, Jackie looked at me and said: "Do you see how that works, kid?" I said: "I sure did!" We were going to be rolling now with this new move.

The other guys on the crew all saw what happened. It wasn't long before they were doing the same stunt except Pete. Pete was a straight laced guy. Each time we would pull the trick, Pete's face would make contortions and his eyeglasses would flop around on his head. He was a nervous wreck. Pete never pulled the move but he had no problem sharing the tips at the end of the shift. He kept his mouth shut and never ratted us out. When Eddie and Tommy saw the move, they couldn't wait to get started. We were all in. This move had a huge cash potential. And it was big. We would pull the move a few times a night and net about $150 per dealer. Then, of course, we would piece off $50 each to Jackie Gums. Now, this doesn't sound like much money in today's terms but back then a hundred bucks is worth about six hundred today. So you can see, we were making some really big scores.

Jackie Gums also taught us a few other things as well. Like, you only make the move on prop bets with big payouts. So, we just made the move on one roll bets. They have the highest payouts. There is no sense taking a risk with a low payout. He taught us not to be too greedy. You make the move only when the time was right and only a few times a shift. This is something hard to teach some guys trying to make a score. They are too impatient. There are going to be plenty of opportunities in an eight hour shift. You can't get too greedy. That is how guys would get caught. In fact, there would be stretches of nights where everything was done by the book. You see, you don't want to draw any suspicion to you or your crew.

As a side light, you didn't have to worry about hustling or phantom bets when Yaba Daba Do hit town. This guy was a real heavyweight whale and I am not talking about how much he weighed. Rather, how much his wallet weighed. He was famous up and down the strip. When he walked through the front door, a buzz would travel all throughout the Casino. I would always pray he would come to my table. One night he actually did. He set the standard for all of the other King Georges out there.

This guy played hard and heavy. The smallest bet he would make was $200 for himself. He loved the prop bets and would constantly post $25 on hard ways and one roll bets. And he never forgot about the dealers. He would post $25 bets for the dealers all of the time. I'll never forget this one night. We made $1250 in tips for each dealer. What a night! It was unbelievable.

Afterwards, you couldn't forget to piece off everybody. First, there was Jackie Gums. He got his $200 from each dealer. Plus on this occasion we had to tip the Floor Boss. You had to approach tipping the Floor Boss a little differently. You couldn't just walk up and hand him some money. No, you had to be just a little slick about tipping him. We always had a lot of money in our pockets. Normally, what I would do is fold up a hundred dollar bill into a little square. Then I would place the folded bill behind the matches in a match book. I would walk up to the podium like I was checking out, because I was, and place the book of matches on the podium. He knew just where to find it. The Floor Boss would just slyly pick up the match book and place it in his pocket.

We had a great night and the word traveled all over the Casino. When I came to work the next day, I parked in the employee lot which had a security guard. It was located directly behind the MGM about a quarter mile away. Then, I would walk through security at the employees' entrance and down the hallway to the Dealers' room. The Dealers' room was where we congregated before we would start our shift. It was next to the Dealers' café. The room had lockers for the dealers. Later on, when I started a brand new move with Jackie Gums, I would store the chips in the locker during break time. I had to put them somewhere! I couldn't be walking around with a pocket full of chips clicking around, could I? It would draw suspicion.

Anyway, the next day walking toward the Dealers' room there was a line of Boxmen waiting for me. Get this, everyone of them had their hand out looking to get pieced off. Some of these guys were on the table for only about ten minutes. I still had to give them something. What a racket these guys would pull.

We had some crew working together. We were more successful than any other crew out there. These other dealers would gossip about us. They were worse than little girls. They were always asking us what we made the night before. I would tell them: "I think we scored $700 in tokes last night. No, that was the night before. Last night we scored $800." I would do it just to give them a hard time. They were only making about a half of what we were taking. They couldn't stand it.

At the end of each shift, we would pick up the Toke Box and bring it over to the counter by the podium inside the Pit. We had ten games going on so, we had a big area with a number of podiums and counters. We would empty the box and count the tips in front of everybody before we brought them to the cage. Thinking back on it, it was a really dumb thing to do. But for some reason, and I think it was an ego thing, we counted the tips so all of the dealers could see how good we were and how much we were making. Little did they know a bunch of the chips were from phantom bets and past posting bets.

One night while we were cutting up the totes, the graveyard shift boss, Sammy Hans comes over and says out loud: "How in the hell does this crew make so much money every single night?" We just ignored him and went about counting. Of course the other dealers would become jealous of us. I mean we were scoring about 80 to 100 percent more than they were. And it was all tax free.

One night before the shift started, Sammy Hans told Tommy Socks and me to see Maury Yeager the Casino Manager. I nearly had a heart attack. The only time a dealer would see him is if they were going to get fired. We went to his office and knocked. He yelled out: "Liosi and Socks. Get in here." It was just the two of us. We went in and sat down. The first thing I said was: "Are you going to fire us? Because, the only time anyone comes in here is when they're getting fired". He ignored me. Then he looked directly at both of us and said: "We've been noticing your crew is doing quite well at generating tokes. You know the both of you are only working here because of your brothers vouching for you. And you know the policy we have about hustling for tokes, don't you? Well make sure we don't catch you hustling or else we will fire you on the spot, brothers or no brothers. Understand?"

I can't remember what I said if I said anything at all. I just remember leaving the office and walking down the hallway. Tommy asked me if we should cool it with the scam we were running. I said, no way. We reported to the Pit and all I could see was Sammy Hans watching us walk across the Casino floor. He knew what the conversation was all about and he wanted us to know we are being watched carefully.

It didn't take long and we were back up running the scam with Jackie Gums at the helm. For the six weeks we were working together as a crew, we made a killing. Between hustling for tips, salary, and the new moves of phantom bets and post betting, we netted about $6000 each. You could buy a brand new corvette for that amount of money. It was a big moment. Like clockwork though, the six weeks passed, and the scheduler broke up our crew. I knew I needed to come up with something else. I was getting used to the money and loving the life style it provided. Then it dawned on me.

Six

MGM - THE AGENT RETURNS

I lost my crew. We were doing great before they broke us up. They assigned me with a new crew with three other guys who were as exciting as paint drying. I mean these guys were real stiffs. See, if you have a great personality, they don't want you. Why? Money! It always comes back to the money. A personable dealer gets tips at the table. The more tips for the dealers, the less money for the casino. So, they stuck me with three other stiffs. These guys were boring and I knew they would just deal as told. I needed to rethink my situation.

I called these guys the "Dead End Crew". I knew I was going to make dead money for the next six weeks. These guys were so bad I knew they wouldn't be able to hustle, steal, or anything. Plus, to make matters worse, the bosses had me on their radar. I should have never counted those tokes in front of everyone. Now it was coming back to bite me. In fact, the very first night with the new crew, Don Larkin, one of the Floor Managers, walked up behind me and whispered in my ear: "Don't even breathe!" I immediately knew what he meant. It means no hustling and no talking to the customers. I had to just stand there like a dummy and deal. We had a term for it, "Keep your head down and your asses up."

It didn't take me long to figure out I needed to make money some other way. Actually, it took me exactly five seconds to figure it out. I had Jackie Gums in my corner so all I had to do is give Uncle Dennis a call. I called him and told him to make sure he has a clean shirt at the gas station so we can start making some moves at the MGM. He was only too happy to hear from me. I also told him we would start right away and use the same routine we used at the Flamingo. He was ready and all too willing.

The next thing I needed to do was to get Jackie in on it. I mean, I knew he would go for it. I just needed to tell him about it. Jackie Gums was a derelict gambler himself. Many times after the shift was over, he would head downtown to the Mint or the Horseshoe and be there all morning at the crap table. In order to feed this habit, he did all sorts of fund raising schemes. Jackie would hustle anything. For starters, he would steal thousands off the table with his false teeth move. On top of that move, he would go to the Pawn Shops downtown and buy jewelry. He would bring the jewelry back to the MGM and sell them to the dealers for double what he paid. Another scheme was to sell butane lighters. He sold them for a buck a piece to the dealers. I'll never forget this one time he got a shipment of lighters from China and the price tags of five cents were still on them. He had his wife and mother in law scrape off the prices so he could go in and sell them for a buck. It was pretty funny. He would do anything to hustle a dollar.

One night as Jackie was sitting at the Boxman position, I cautiously told him I had an Agent and was planning to bring him in. He looked at me and said: "That's okay by me. Tell me when you are ready."

Then he said: "No prop bets, no hustling, no phantom bets, and no post betting, understand? Just hand it off and make place bets as well." He was one of the sharpest guys out there. I knew exactly what he was talking about. I was really excited and knew we were going to pass some big stuff off. Plus he could think on his feet. One time he was doing his cop the chips in his gum act right before break. As he got up to leave, the Floor Boss came over and asked him a question about a credit player. Of course, Jackie's mouth was full of black chips! What does he do? He acts like he is having a heart attack and needing some water. The Floor Boss goes to get the water giving Jackie enough time to move the chips to his suit coat. He was brilliant!

The next day I called Uncle Dennis. He was ready. He actually showed up with a nice, cleanly pressed white dress shirt. Of course, his hands were a little greasy and he smelled a little of gas, but that was okay. Jackie Gums was so sharp, he spotted the Agent about 20 feet away walking to the table. Jackie turned to me and said: "Looks like your friend has arrived." I just went about my business dealing. That's how sharp Jackie was. It is one thing to have a Boxman working with you but it is quite something else when you have a really intelligent, cunning Boxman working with you. He knew the right times and was really observant of what is going on. He knew when to cool it and when to attack. He was amazing. We were going to make some real money working together.

We started to make our major moves. First of all, we graduated from reds to strictly greens and blacks. Why risk it with only reds? We wanted some real cash. One of the best smooth move we had was simply pass the chips to the rail. It is a little harder to do today the way the tables are configured. But then, if you worked second base, the rail right next to you was open and close. It took nothing to simply take a stack of greens and just place them in the rail for Uncle Dennis who was standing there. Then Dennis would place the stack in his pocket. Remember, it has to be done when the dice are flying down the far side of the table. Everybody is looking at the dice and nobody is looking at me. This was a consistent winning score.

Then there was this other great move. When Uncle Dennis showed up, and with all of the confusion at the table, I would put $1500 worth of place bets for him across the board. He never placed any money. I would just take a stack and make the place bets for him. When the numbers came out, I just paid him as normal. It was pure profit since the bets made were casino money. Then if a 'seven out' happened, I would just turn to Dennis and say: "Your bets were off were they not Mr. C.?" Off course he would say: "Yes." And with a stroke of genius, I would take all of his place bets down, stack the blacks up, slide the stack to the Come section of the table, and then match it with another stack of blacks. With this one move, we stole $3000.

There is no need to draw any attention to your self after a big score like this one. We all knew the move was over and Uncle Dennis knew. So he would softly walk to the cage to cash out. Sometimes other players would notice what we did. It did not register to them right away since the game was moving so fast. Once it dawned on them, they would shake their head and be back to the game. They really didn't care and they thought we just screwed up.

The key is you have to have a jammed up table with plenty of players and plenty of bets flying. That was the trick. And when you did hit the Casino, you did it fast and furious and called it quits the rest of the night. There were three of us on this score so the split became 25% for Uncle Dennis, 25% for Jackie Gums and 50% for me. I told Dennis I had to pay off the Floor Boss. I kept that share. In this one night, I made $1500 for myself. The next day, I pulled up to the gas station where Uncle Dennis worked. I got out of the car and said: "Fill it up!" He knew what I meant.

We normally worked Table Ten right in front of the Baccarat Pit. This one night we had a junket in from Los Angeles. The table was packed. On one of the throws we had a cocked die. A cocked die is when the die lands and leans on a stack of chips or the wall. The standard rule is for the far side to be called. Well this night the die was lying with a four facing the players and a concealed six. The other die was a one. The stickman called a seven out and the dealer at third base picked up the chip stack and the four side fell over revealing a winner five. The players went nuts. I mean there were blacks all over the table. They were screaming like raving lunatics. Then they started picking up the table to turn it over. I never saw anything like it. Just then Arty Yeager who was the Pit Boss starts to leave the pit. Tony Tarkasilo who was about six foot five and at least two hundred and eighty pounds started running our way. He was from Steubenville, Ohio. He went around the game and announced: "Put everybody's bet back up on the game." We did. But you know many of the customers exaggerated their bet amounts. Then he said: "Pay everybody on the line!" We did. Tony knew the casino would get it back. These gamblers were here for the weekend and they planned on playing all weekend. In the end, the Casino would get it all back.

It was the early seventies and cocaine was starting to hit town in a big way. You knew the Casino employees were prime targets. In fact, I had my first introduction to coke from Lorenzo. He was working on the Dead End Crew with me. One night he asked me what I did on my night off. I told him the normal. Go out to eat, drink, and see a show somewhere. He then handed me a little packet of white powder. I asked him what it was and he told me take a snort of it if you feel tired or just out to have a good time. This was one of the biggest mistakes I ever made and regret it to this day. He knew I was susceptible and would eventually get hooked to it. And he was right. At this point, I was not too much into it but all that would change. Coke can ruin people's lives.

For example, there was this one dealer, Willie D., who I met at the Flamingo. Although he would screw up all of the time and come to work high all of the time, he would never get fired because he was juiced in. I mean he was always high on coke. Well, there was this Boxman from the Stardust called Al D. He would come over the Flamingo all of the time. He and Willie would disappear for a while. Sometimes I would see them talking off to the side. You know what was going on there. Al was never high, so he must have been making a delivery. Hymie was still at the Stardust and I knew he was definitely connected to the mob. Al D. worked at the Stardust as well so I thought he probably had a similar connection. I can't prove it but I suspected the mob was moving on Vegas with the drugs. It just seemed to connect. Al D. would come over, meet with Willie who was a degenerate drug abuser, and leave shortly thereafter. It seemed he was using Willie to sell drugs.

When the MGM opened, Al D. moved over as a Boxman with a whole ton of other dealers from the Stardust. I think the mob was trying to infiltrate the MGM. At the same time, Willie moved to the MGM as well. One night, Al and a Shift Boss named George

Racha were done their shift and leaving to walk over to the Barbary Coast parking lot. No sooner were they out the door than a security guy came out and called George back to the MGM. Al continued to walk to his car and Willie was waiting for him. He shot Al five times with a handgun. Al died on the spot. Had George been there, he would have been killed too. Apparently there was some big problem with the drugs and money. Since Willie was coked up all of the time, you know he was not thinking straight. The cops caught up to him at some preacher's house. I wasn't really sure what happened to him. The rumor was he went to prison for life. This is what cocaine can do to you.

There were always great looking women at the MGM especially after the shows let out. Our table was in perfect position to see the parade of women of the night walk by. I had this bad habit of saying "psst" to them as they walked by our table. I did it to get their attention. One time, this one woman with a low cut black gown was walking by. She was beautiful. As normal, I "psst" her. She stopped dead in her stride to find out who made the sound. Just then Morey, a Floor Boss, walked dead into her. He was totally embarrassed. He stomped into the Pit to the podium and met with the other Floor Bosses. Next thing I know they take me off the pole and send me to break.

While I was at break, they asked the Dead End Crew who made the sound. At first, they acted like they didn't know. Then Morey told them he would fire the whole crew if they didn't tell him who made the sound. The Dead End Crew turned me in. I came back from break and Morey came over to me and told me I was fired. That was the end of my days at the MGM. I had a good run and I knew they had the crosshairs on me. I needed to move on to something new.

Can't believe the Starboard is still around.

Seven

Four Queens, Paradise And Royal LV

I worked with Tommy Capp as a bartender back in Cleveland. He and I were buddies. He heard what happened to me at the MGM and gave me a call. He told me they needed a bartender at the Starboard Tack where he was and I could start right away. He knew I had bartender experience. I needed a job so I said I could start right now and I did. It was 1977. I was pretty well off financially but I still needed a steady income. The Starboard was a pretty classy place. It was the first place in town to offer surf and turf. It was located on Sahara and Atlantic. Today this area is pretty dicey. It is made up of car dealerships and run down areas with dope deals. Back in the day, it was a hopping spot like many areas close to the strip.

Meanwhile, my brother, Paulie, moved to Atlantic City to train dealers for Casears. Before he left, he gave me his black book. He had about ten steady customers who borrowed money from him paying about 3 to 5 percent interest a week. He sold me the customers for what they borrowed from him. Now, I started into the Shylocking business. I had about five dealers at the Caesars and five poker dealers over at the Stardust. So, I worked as a bartender and started making money lending out. Soon I would embark on a new business.

The Starboard was run by two brothers named Bill and Steve Cookie. These guys were heavy into coke. They asked me to come into their office one day and there were lines of coke laying on the desk. They asked me to do a line. They were testing me to see if I was a rat and just to feel me out. I did a line and I could see them nod to each other. At this point, I started to get more into the drug racket.

One night this Italian guy, Tony Pro, who was a regular customer, came into the bar area to see me.

His day job was a court reporter downtown. He asked me if I would meet him at his house to share some coke. I started to get into it so I was happy to get a good source and a free hit. His place was close to the strip and easy to get to. In fact, during this time, the town was not very big. You could get around very easily. I pulled up to his place and we met. He suggested selling me some coke and I could resell it at the bar. Also, he asked if I was willing to make some deliveries. He said he would pay me $500 a week plus he would sell me Quaaludes at $1.50 each pill. I could easily get $3 a piece for them. I thought about it. This was a great opportunity to get a steady supply of both coke and Quaaludes. It would also be a good money maker. So, I told him I was interested.

I started right away. I only needed to make 10 deliveries a week. Each delivery would consist of 100 pills. I started to sell coke on the side as well. From the bartender gig, selling coke and Quaaludes, and my Shylocking business, I was pulling in some big money. I did this for about a year when I got a call from Jose Cuban. He was a dealer in the Baccarat Pit at Caesars. He was robbing them blind at the time plus he was borrowing money from me. Not only was he a big coke user, he was also a degenerate gambler.

He knew my history and my schemes. He had a good contact at the Four Queens. He made me a deal. I would wipe the loan clean and he would get me a Boxman job at the Four Queens. It sounded like a great plan to me. I knew how well Jackie Gums did as a Boxman. Afterall, he taught me all of the moves so it sounded enticing. I quit my bartender job. The meet with the two brothers had importance and will come in later.

Jose put me in touch with a guy named Vern. Vern was the Floor Boss on the Swing Shift. Also, Jose told me: "Vern is all too happy to work with you". I knew what he meant! I started right away and started wearing a suit to work. It didn't take any time at all and Vern approached me and asked me if I had an Agent. I told him I sure did. Now remember, downtown you got mostly racetrack types who were small bettors. All of the heavy bettors were down on the strip. Vern had a new move though. I never thought of it and it would make us a ton of money.

They just started doing credit downtown. It was new and not very sophisticated. The Floor Manager would simply keep a pad of paper in his pocket. Whenever someone needed credit and he knew him to be good for it, he would simply write down the player's name, date, and amount of credit issued. The slip would eventually make it to the cage where they kept track. Vern came up to me and told me to bring in my Agent. He told me to give him a little direction on who the agent is when he arrives. This was easy to do.

I called the gas station and Dennis showed up in no time. As soon as he came to the table I nodded to Vern. Vern came over and pulled out his pad from his pocket. He then instructed me to give Dennis $200 in chips on credit. I looked back and said: "No way! He's getting $300" which I proceeded to give him. I wasn't going to take a risk for only sixty five bucks which is the three way split. I thought Vern was going to have a fit. He started to turn red. But he let it go since it was too late. I already pushed the chips over to Uncle Dennis.

Now, this is where the move comes in. Vern has his pen and he makes it look like he is writing on the credit marker pad. But in reality, he isn't writing a thing. He is faking it. He never wrote anything down. There was no marker! He would pass the pad over to Uncle Dennis for his signature and he would fake like he was signing the marker as well. It was a terrific scheme. Meanwhile, Uncle Dennis would make a couple of bets and then it was off to the cage to cash in. This move was terrific. I never thought of it. In fact, most of the moves I didn't come up with by myself. I was always taught how to do it by experienced Boxmen and Dealers. We would pull this move off about four times a week. I had to split it three ways. After doing it four times a week, it would add up to about $400 each. Not a bad additional pay check. I was happy with the split.

This was my first job on the box. I was thinking about how I could make some additional moves on my own. Well! I remembered Jackie Gums. I just needed to make his moves. And the best one is to help the dealers clean off the table. So, I started to help the dealers out. At first they thought it was strange but they got used to it. You know I was going to start cupping chips. Working at the MGM, I had plenty of practice. I had normal teeth so I couldn't use Jackie Gum's false teeth move. So, I did the next best thing. I would just fold my arms in front of me and drop the chips in my inside suit pocket. It worked like a charm. I would make this move about twice a night with one to two greens. I kept to the greens because the Four

Queens is a low end Casino. There were not many blacks out on the layout. After I collected a stack of chips doing this move, I needed a way to cash them in. I couldn't' go to the cage because it would be too suspicious. So, the next best thing was to use Uncle Dennis to cash the chips in for me. I paid him a 20% cut for everything he cashed in for me. It was a great setup.

Another benefit of working the box is you get a great opportunity to handle the cash. The normal procedure when a player wants chips is for him or her to put his cash on the felt. Then the dealer moves the money over to me. I would spread the money out in front of me. I would then pass over the chips to the dealer for the money. After a few seconds, I would move the cash over to the paddle and drop the money in the drop box. It was a pretty basic procedure. Now with this new move, I would only use it on hundred dollar bills. You see, if you are going to take a chance, you need a big payoff. After I did the fan out of cash for the camera, I would take the bill and pull it back to the paddle. The only difference is, the paddle would not put the money in the drop box. Instead, I would slip the bill into my hand as I was placing the paddle in the drop box. And when the time was right, I would put the bill in my inside suit pocket. It was smooth. I got the hang of making it one clean, quiet placement to my pocket. I would do this move a couple times a night for another $200 bonus.

Between Vern with the fake credit slips, slipping chips in my pocket and now slipping cash in my pocket, I was making a pretty good score every week. Things were going good even at a dump like the Four Queens.

As time went on though, I think the Casino Manager, Pete, suspected I was stealing. The golden rule about getting away with stealing is not to get too greedy. Sooner or later the greed will catch up with you. Too much greed will always get you caught. I was getting too greedy. We were working the marker scam. I was cleaning chips off of the table and when the opportunity presented I would swipe a hundred dollar bill or two. One night, I was passing some chips to my inside pocket when I missed. Four green chips fell to the floor. I reached down, picked them up and put them in the stack on the table. I swear the eye or one of the Pit Bosses spotted me. Plus there were these two guys at the table. I knew they saw me make the move. Suddenly, the two guys left the table and never returned. They could have been plants for the casino looking for dealers cheating. These Casino guys knew the tricks and they always kept their eyes open. I knew I screwed up and may have been caught.

About two days later, I was sitting on the box and playing it cool. Just then, someone behind me reached over to my shoulder and announced: "Gaming Commission!" I nearly had a heart attack. My heart dropped to the bottom of my stomach. The guy behind me told me he wanted to inspect the dice. I collected the dice and presented them to him. He looked them over and measured them. He gave them back to me and the game resumed. I think maybe Pete put the Commission up to it to scare me straight. It didn't work. It wasn't long until I was back at it.

A few days later, I was working as normal. Suddenly, Pete came up from behind and said: "Neal. You have to go. We can't afford you anymore. You have to go home." I now knew they had me. They caught me red handed. But why they didn't have me arrested and sent to jail? I don't know why for sure. Maybe, I think, Pete liked me. Or maybe it was honor among thieves.

Everybody was stealing in one form or another at the time. That was it for me at the Four Queens. I stood up immediately and walked out. I told Pete "Thanks" before I left. I knew he could have called Metro and had me booked. Not only would I go to jail, I would be in the famous black book. I would never be able to get a job at a Casino again. I was lucky.

Paradise Casino

Although I was making plenty of money from selling drugs and my Shylocking business, I still needed to make more. The Howard Johnson Hotel on Tropicana Ave just went through bankruptcy. A Boss over at the Riviera decided to buy it and rename it the Paradise. Paradise is the name of the unincorporated town where the strip is located. You see Las Vegas really starts at Sahara Ave going north although the whole strip is named Las Vegas. The location of the hotel was great. It was right next to the strip behind the Tropicana Hotel. They were opening a small casino in the front of the hotel. Now that I had experience as a Boxman, I went down for an interview. Can you believe they put me on the graveyard shift and made me the Floor Boss? Here I was robbing casino after casino and getting another promotion.

The place was a small gambling joint. We had only three 21 games and one craps game. So, I pretty much watched the action. The dice game was run by the dealers only. There was no Boxman or Floor Supervisor at the table. The Casino tried to get some customers in by running buses to and from L.A. but for the most part it was pretty small. This has its disadvantages for a guy like me. Being a Floor Boss, I would supervise the games. This means I couldn't get my hands on the chips. So what did I do? I looked for any excuse to sit down on the crap game and be the Boxman. Whenever there were a lot customers and the action was hot, I would sit down and manage the game. This gave me the chance to go back to my old tricks. I spent most of the time cupping chips to my suit pockets. The game was too small to do any real passing to an Agent. So I stuck to stealing some greens whenever I could.

One time my younger brother, Freddie, came in from Cleveland for a small vacation. I gave him a crash course in taking chips off of the table. He came to play one night and I had him position next to the dealer. Every so often, I would pass a stack over to him. He would take it off the table as planned. After the night was over he had $1500 in chips. Just to show you how small this joint was, he went to the cage and they couldn't cash him in. They didn't have enough money in the cage. They had to go around and empty the drop boxes in order to get the money to pay him. It was hilarious.

For the next six months, I did my job and grabbed some greens when possible. One night about five in the morning, there were only a couple of players. I spotted one credit player and thought he would go along with my dealer bet move. So, I placed two greens on a hard eight. Sure enough the two bets hit. I stacked up two columns of greens and offered one to the customer and the other to the dealers. For some reason, the customer turned down the stack. He turned down a free couple hundred bucks! So, I just shook my head and put the stack in my inside pockets.

The next thing I know, I was called to the Shift Manager's office. I went inside and he was sitting behind the desk. He asked me if I had any chips in my pockets. I told him I sure did. I told him I got quite a few tips that night. He told me to put the chips on the desk which I did. He looked me directly in the eye and told me: "You'll never work in another casino again as long as I am around." I was just fired, again.

Turns out the Philadelphia Mob was running the Paradise and they were gutting it. They were running a credit scam which drained the hotel of all of their cash. Here I thought Vern and I were the only ones who knew the credit scam. The Philly Mob was doing the same thing but in a much bigger way. They were running all kinds of credit moves where they would get the hotel management to get extended credit from liquor distributors to the company who made the cocktail napkins. Plus they were skimming the hotel. It finally was forced to go into bankruptcy.

Royal Las Vegas

Vegas was still a small town of about 200,000 people. Word gets around fast in such a small town and especially within the industry. I would work out at this gym where I met Big Al. This guy was about 240 pounds of muscle. When I would see him at the gym, we would spot each other lifting weights. He worked over at the Royal Las Vegas. The Royal Las Vegas was a casino on Convention Center Drive. Next door to it was the Royal Inn. The Cleveland mob owned both places and all of the wise guys would hang out at the casino and stay at the hotel. Big Al was a 21 and roulette dealer there. He told me he could get me juiced in if I wanted. I needed a job so I said okay.

Before you know it, I was working as a Boxman on the crap table. I went back to my old ways of stealing chips. I had a chance to meet these two guys named JT and Wendell. JT worked the craps table. He only had four fingers on one hand. His thumb was missing. I never asked him what happened but I think it involved the mob. Even without a thumb, he was one of the best craps dealers of all time. He really knew his way around the table. Wendell on the other hand was the Floor Boss. He had false teeth. I found out because he came in to work one day with no teeth. Turns out he and JT were out drinking the night before and Wendell left his teeth at one of the bars. Of course, he didn't know which one. So he had to call all of the places he was the night before asking if his teeth were there. It was pretty funny.

It became pretty clear to me these two guys were associated with the Cleveland mob and they were there to watch things. Big Al gave me a good word so they started me right away. They put me on the Box at first. Then I think they spotted me stealing chips because they promoted me to Floor Boss. They didn't want to get rid of me. I think they were helping themselves as well and wanted me to be in a position where I was not handling cash or chips. I worked for a while. I looked for every opportunity to get on the box especially if it was a jammed game. But it was hard to get on those games. They really wanted me to stay Floor Boss.

I was there about six months and I took a ski trip up to Lake Tahoe. I was having a great time and wanted to extend the trip by a few days. So, I called Wendell and asked him for a few extra days. He told me to take all the time I wanted. They were shutting down the Royal Las Vegas. The Cleveland Mob decided to gut the hotel and casino. The mob in Vegas generally wanted an ongoing casino operation so they could keep a good skim going. Some other ones just wanted to steal as much as possible and walk away. That was the case with the Paradise and Royal Las Vegas. They got what they could and then they shut it down. A few weeks later I ran into JT at Café Michelle. He said hello and told me he hoped I got as much as possible out of the Royal as he did. He knew I was stealing. But so was he. I couldn't believe I was stealing from the mob.

Salvatories was the best Italian Restaurant in Town. All the stars went there to eat.

Eight

SALVATORIES

It wasn't long before I got a call from an old friend named Salvator. He was an Italian guy. He was actually born in the old country. We all called him Sal for short. I first met Sal at the Flamingo. We worked there together. He was mostly on the 21 and Baccarat tables. He was robbing the casino blind. Remember, the Baccarat table still dealt with cash on the table. Even though he was stealing a ton of money, he was a really bad gambler. I inherited him as a mark from my brother's black book. He was a nice guy and always paid on time. We were actually friends. I brought him over to UNLV to see his very first football game. One day he asked me to come over to his place for dinner.

Man, this guy could cook. I was there for two hours. It was the best Italian food I ever had. He told me he was thinking about opening a place on Sahara. I told him with food like this, it would be a big hit.

Sure enough, he and his wife opened a small restaurant called the Italian Kitchen on West Sahara. You could fit about 30 people in the joint. It didn't take long for the word to get out and the customers came rolling in. He stole enough money from the Flamingo to bankroll the place. It was the best Italian food in town. Everybody would go there including all of the celebrities who came to town. It wasn't long before he started filling up the wall with autograph photos from the entertainers. He was on my list so I would do my weekly visit to pick up the juice. This one time I visited, guess who was there as well? Tony the Ant from the Chicago Mob! What was he doing there? We were both there to pick up the juice. Turns out Tony the Ant and his Hole in the Wall gang would eat there often. Somehow, Sal borrowed money from him and he was there to collect.

This was before they were known as the Hole in the Wall Gang. They were famous for stealing anything they could get their hands on. They got their name from burglarizing stores by drilling holes in the wall or in the roof. Whatever they stole, they would sell in their storefront called the Gold Rush. As chance may have it, the gang was caught drilling a hole in a store across the street called Berthas. I always wondered if they were casing the place when they were eating at the Gourmet. Tony the Ant wasn't there during the robbery so he didn't get caught or convicted for it.

There I was standing right next to Tony the Ant making my collections. He didn't say much. Just hello and he walked off. Meanwhile, Sal was telling me he was doing a great business and was thinking about opening a bigger place. I told him it was a great idea. Vegas was not big. So, where ever he opened a place, you can bet the word would get out and the crowds would follow. He heard about the Royal Las Vegas shutting down and he asked me if I would be interested in being a bartender. I said sure. My loan business and drug dealing certainly would keep me afloat while I waited for him to open his new place.

While waiting for Sal to open his new place, I got a bartender gig working with the Cookie brothers. They called this new restaurant the Port Tack as a spinoff of the Starboard Tack. These two guys were more concerned about a front for their drug dealing business than running a restaurant. I needed to earn some extra bucks so I called them and asked if I could bartend. They already knew I wouldn't rat them out from before, so they put me to work. What a nest of thieves this place turned out to be. Everybody was stealing. The Valet guys were robbing anything you left in the car and the waiters were stealing every chance they got. Get a load of how their scam worked. Back then, a lot of people still paid in cash. So, whenever a customer paid in cash it was like an alarm went off telling the waiters their time has arrived. At the time, all restaurants would use the paper pads to take your order and give you the bill. There was nothing electronic. So what the waiters did was to start by putting a small hole in the wall back by the kitchen. Then when they had a cash customer they would drop the order slips in the wall and keep the cash payment along with their tip. What a racket. Of course the maître de knew what was going on. So, the waiters would have to kick back to him to keep him quiet. The Cookie brothers were so high all the time and wrapped up in their drug business they didn't seem to care or pay attention. They were making so much money selling drugs, it covered all losses in the restaurant. Years later, they were renovating the place and taking down some of the walls. When they were renovating in the kitchen, out comes thousands and I mean thousands of order slips from the wall. By this time, everyone was long gone so there was no going after them. I had the bartender job feeding the drinks to the wait staff. So, I didn't get much of a chance to pocket any money. But the waiters took good care of me since they knew I knew what was going on.

Before you know it, Sal was able to open a new place on Paradise road. He called it Salvatories. If you wanted to be seen and see the celebrities as well, this was the place to be. Everybody who was anybody went there. After all, he had the best food in town. I asked Sal how he got the money to open the place especially since he was still paying me juice. I knew he made a killing at the Flamingo but I couldn't imagine how he could bankroll a place like this. Sure enough, he had to get a partner named Freddie Meyer. Freddie was connected to the mob and he owned a gym in town called the Sports Club. Everybody seemed to go to this gym. And when you are connected, you get all the mobsters, wiseguys, and their associates to go there as well. I asked Sal if he knew anything about

Freddie. He said he did and he said he had no choice because he needed the start up money.

When Savatories opened up, Freddie and Sal comped all the meals for the first two days. What a way to open a place! All of the waiters, cooks, bartenders, etc. worked for free and took only tips. Sal brought a whole crew of cooks in from Italy to work there as well. Sal would work with the crew from Italy in the kitchen and they put out the best food anywhere in town. Everybody would come to Salvatories for dinner. We had lawyers from downtown Las Vegas, politicians would come, the Mayor, the Governor when he was in town, businessmen, wives, professional athletes, girls of the night, and even the UNLV basketball team. Some of the great celebrities included Paul Anka, Debbie Reynolds, Bill Russell, James Caan, Telly Savalis, just to name a few. And since Freddie was connected, all of his wiseguy friends would come in. Tony the Ant's gang were regulars as well as a whole host of other underworld types paying loyalty to the place. If the mob had a place in town, it was a rule their associates would pay homage. So, we had a steady stream of mobsters coming in. And if you get mobsters, you get law enforcement as well.

Sal did most of the real work. He put in 16 hour days in the kitchen. He liked his wine. So, he would consume about a gallon of wine everyday. It didn't seem to phase him though. Freddie was actually the front man for the real guys who put the money up. So, he was always out front managing the employees. The employees hated him. He was mean and treated people very poorly. He thought he was a big shot and talked to the employees in very derogatory terms. The employees couldn't do anything or else they would get fired. We made good money with the tips and there were plenty of customers so we just took the abuse. Freddie liked to be a big man in front of everyone and was always buying people drinks or comping dinners. He used to love to comp celebrities and the men's UNLV basketball team. Meanwhile, Sal was back in the kitchen slaving away. Sal was in a bad position because he was paying juice to the mob for his loans and he had the mob as a partner. It was a pretty bad arrangement.

Meanwhile, Tony the Ant was able to infiltrate the Tropicana through a Casino Manager named Tommy Karney. Using Tommy Karney, they were able to bilk millions from the Trop through skimming, bad credit, no credit scams, etc.. They even had a scam involving the Valet guys. When a customer would arrive at the Valet, they would greet you nicely and ask you if you were staying the weekend and if you needed the car. They would tell you they needed to park the cars father away for people not needing access to their vehicle. Then, when the customer was checking in, the Valet would call Tony. The Ant and his crew would arrive to the Trop, get the keys from the Valet, and drive the customer's car to their house to rob it. They would know where the person lived from the registration in the car. And here's the best part. When they were robbing the house, the homeowner's car would be in the driveway. So, the neighbors wouldn't think anything strange was going on. What a scam. The next thing you know, the customer's jewelry would be on sale at the Gold Rush and the Valet guy would get a couple hundred for the tip.

The FBI was constantly trying to tie Tony the Ant and Tommy Karney to the skim at the Trop. One night I was working the bar and a FBI agent came up to me and gave me his card. He asked me if I saw Tommy Karney. I told him he was eating. The FBI guy told me to go over and let him know they were here. He said they would wait for him in the front booth. So, I told a waiter to go over and let Tommy

K. know the FBI wanted to talk to him. Tommy came up to me and asked where they were. I told him they were in the front booth. Tommy K. told me to send them over a drink. I did and the FBI guys sent it back. Then the FBI guys got up and went over to Tommy K. at the bar. They said a few words to Tommy and they left. The FBI was just busting on Tommy and wanted him to know they were on his trail. You would think this was unusual but it wasn't. Salvatories was a big hang out for the wiseguys. So, the cops would come in often just to say hello.

My supplier of drugs was still Tony Pro. I still had the route he set up and he was giving me a steady supply of coke and Quaaludes. All of a sudden, he started hanging out at the Bar at Salvatories. At first, I didn't think anything of it. I couldn't really say anything because I didn't want to burn my supplier. I would talk to Tony whenever he came. He told me he did a stint in prison for a previous drug bust. He said he spent two years. I just listened. As time went on, he started asking me questions about the coke customers I had. He would ask things like what their names were, where they lived, stuff like that. I avoided giving any answers but it started to raise suspicion. Did he want to steal my customers away? Was he being a rat for the Feds? Was he there keeping an eye on the wiseguys for the FBI? Was he some kind of plant? I wasn't really sure at this point but I started to suspect something.

One day I came into work and I saw Sal at the front door. This was strange since he was usually in the kitchen. I asked him what was going on and he said we were robbed. I looked around and all of the booze was gone. There was not one single bottle behind the bar. Everything was missing. We had a wine cellar stocked full with some really expensive fine wines. Every bottle was missing. They cleaned the place out. Plus, the safe was missing. They even took the bowl of candies we had at the end of the bar. The funny thing was, there was no forced entry anywhere. It was like someone had the keys and let themselves in. Sal already met with the cops and the insurance company earlier in the day and filled out the reports. It was strange to see such a sight. With about 30 minutes left to open, Sal and I were discussing what to do. Should we open? Should we open without the liquor and just serve food? As we were talking, guess who pulls up? Freddie Meyer shows up with a crew of guys and a truck load full of liquor and wine. He walked up and told us to open as normal. He would have the wine cellar and bar stocked in no time. And he did it. The bar was stocked with new full bottles of liquor and the cellar was completely full of new bottles of wine. Later in the evening, I asked Sal if he told Freddie about the robbery. He said he didn't tell him because he couldn't get a hold of him. Sal said he was the one who discovered the robbery. I looked at Sal and he looked at me with the same look of a light bulb going off in our heads. I said, if nobody told Freddie, how did he know to show up and restock the bar? The answer became pretty clear to us. These mob guys will do anything to extract a buck out of an operation. The insurance paid the claim. The restaurant got a check for $5,000 for the missing booze and a $35,000 check for the money which was in the safe. Some score, huh. You will always find one consistent trait with any business the mob owns. They always pay their insurance premiums on time.

You just knew Freddie had something to do with this heist. But we were up and running the same evening. We didn't miss a meal. Freddie always thought of himself as a big shot and had a huge ego. He had us all refer to him as Mr. M. He also had us get all comps approved by getting his signature on a comp sheet he created. I think he liked the idea of us coming over asking for his signature. Plus, he loved to be a big shot and hand out comps. Sal asked him to slow down the comps but Freddie would announce he was charging $3.50 for a drink which cost him 50 cents. So, he would always say he didn't care. I remember once going up to him to get a comp signature when he was sitting next to Paul Anka. Paul thought I was coming up for an autograph and started rolling his eyes. It was hilarious when I approach Freddie and asked for his approval on a comp sheet. It was really funny and everybody laughed.

Now, Sal was a thief robbing the Flamingo during his Baccarat Dealer days. So, he naturally thought everybody else was a thief as well. He wasn't half wrong though. He got quite paranoid about people beating him out of money. So much so, I would see him in the back going through the garbage looking for food checks which may have been tossed by a waiter. He thought the waiters were tossing out food checks and pocketing the dinner service money. Meanwhile Big Shot Freddie was the one handing out everything for free. Sal's paranoia never seemed to end. Even though he was in the kitchen all the time, he would come out to check on the waiters, check on me, and look in the register. I think all the wine he was drinking was making him crazy. He would take a gallon jug of wine, mix it with water and drink it all day and night. He would go through at least one gallon a day. It was really distorting his thought patterns. One day he suspected I was beating him out of money in the bar area. He didn't even wait for me to come in to work. He called me on the phone and fired me. He just told me he had to let me go. That was it. No real explanation. Funny thing is I never stole a penny when I worked at Salvatories. I thought we were friends. Since he fired me, I asked him to pay off his loan he had with me. He did pay it off. He most likely borrowed more from Tony the Ant. Here I was out of a job again.

I almost got busted here on the 5th floor.

Nine

Drugs – The End

It wasn't long before I got a call from Tony Pro. He hanged out at the bar in Salvatores so he knew I got fired. He asked me to do some more stops for him. I had time on my hands so it was no problem. I was working with this guy named Jimmie Smith. He was fired along with twenty one other dealers from the Sands. We started doing the deals together. We used his safe at his house to store the coke and ludes. He also had a sports car in the garage which just sat there. So, we used it as a storage place for the drugs as well. We would keep the dope in the trunk.

One of the stops was off of Harmon. There was this gas station and next to it was an alley. In the alley was a dumpster. I would place the dope behind the dumpster. I used to ride my bicycle a lot making deliveries. This one day I was making the delivery at the dumpster and I saw two cars with two guys in each car one at each end of the alley. They just stopped there and they were looking at me. My heart dropped. I knew I was going to get busted. I had about 500 pills on me. There was no way I could escape. Then something really strange happened. Both cars drove away. I couldn't understand it. Why would they corner me and then drive away? Maybe they were just scoping out the drop point. I didn't see them following me. I don't know what happened for sure. I didn't make the drop and drove my bike back to Jimmie's place. I told him what happened and he couldn't make anything out of it either.

The next day Tony Pro called me and asked what happened. I told him and he said he wanted to meet with me at Café Michelle. It was located on Maryland and Flamingo. This was a popular place especially with the mob. The wiseguys would hang out there during the day getting lunch and discussing their next scam. Tony asked to meet him at 5 pm. I went over and he was sitting at the bar. I walked up to him and he asked me to sit down. He then asked me where the drugs were from the missed drop. I told him I had it on me. He kept asking me if I had his back and I told him I did. Just then these two giant detectives walked in. These two guys were about 6'5" each and weighed about 290 pounds each. They immediately came over to where we were sitting and took out their guns. They took Tony Pro to the ground, cuffed him and arrested him. Meanwhile I am sitting there with the drugs in my pocket. They told me to get out of the way. I did and they left with Tony Pro. I couldn't believe what happened. I could have got pinched again in a matter of two days.

Turns out, Tony Pro thought the guy who missed the pick up stole the dope. So what did Tony do? This nut job went over to the guy's house and kidnapped his girlfriend. He took her at gun point and brought her to his house where he held her against her will. The guy called the cops, told them about missing the dope pick up, told them his girlfriend was missing, and he was dealing with Tony Pro. The cops immediately went over to Tony Pros house and found her tied to the bed. Can you believe this? Over a small drug deal, he goes nutty and kidnaps somebody. The cops weren't going to stand for this so they put him away. I don't know how many years he got. I never heard from him again.

I was using more and more of the coke and I was losing control. I couldn't hold a job for more than a few weeks. I was getting more and more paranoid. I kept thinking I was going to get pinched. And since Tony Pro was out of the scene, I lost my supplier. Now I became the buyer instead of the seller. I was always wondering where I could get my next high. Plus I started to have a cash flow problem. The drugs can make you do crazy things and once you are hooked, you are hooked forever. I became hooked.

I still had about 3000 Quaalude pills I could deal. I had them in Jimmie's car trunk. I stopped over his place and told him I had a buyer for 2000 pills over at the apartment building on Sahara. I found this buyer through Tony Pro when I was making his deliveries. So, I got the pills and went over about 8 pm to do the deal. The apartment was on the fifth floor. When I walked in there was about four people there. I dealt with them in the past but something seemed odd and out of place. They had some coke lines on the kitchen table and asked me if I wanted a line. I said sure and did a quick line. I didn't stay long. I got my money then left for the elevator. When the elevator door opened there were two Metro Cops standing in it! I wasn't sure what to do. I couldn't run because there was nowhere to run to. The cops were not getting off. They were just standing there. I had no choice but to walk on the elevator. My heart was pounding a million times a second. Although I delivered the 2000 pills, I had the other 1000 pills on me for another stop I was going to do. I stepped into the elevator. The cops didn't get out and they didn't have a floor button pushed. I selected the first floor. I was sure they were going to arrest me. I was scared to death. When we got to the first floor, the elevator doors opened and I walked out. I tried to stay calm on the outside but inside I was having a heart attack. The cops stayed on the elevator!

I went across the street to watch to see if anything would happen. Sure enough the cops came out with the four people in cuffs. The cops busted them! Why didn't they arrest me? I stood and thought for a minute. I had a few problems to deal with. I was spared from getting arrested in the alley. Then they didn't arrest me when I was with Tony Pro at the bar. And now, I wasn't arrested this time on a delivery. They had me cold each time and they didn't do anything. Why? Plus I had the added problem of these four guys getting arrested. They probably think I was a snitch. They would most likely try to get revenge on me. Then it dawned on me. The light bulb finally went off in my head. Tony Pro was an informant for the cops. No wonder why he kept asking me detailed questions about the dope deals. I knew he went to jail before. I'm thinking he probably got busted again and the cops flipped him as an informant. How else could it be explained? I realized the cops were following me and I was leading them to all these busts. They had enough of Tony with the kidnapping and had to take him off the street. Now, I was really scared. It was only a matter of time for me to get pinched. Plus, if Tony is out of the scene the cops are either going to flip me or pinch me. I was in a dangerous situation.

After thinking about the possibility of getting busted and the other dopers getting revenge on me, I knew I had no choice. I headed directly to the airport and took the first flight to San Diego. My time had run out in Vegas. I was too lucky and I knew I had to get away. I had money from the drug deal to get me started. So, I got a place on Coronado Beach. I called my wife and told her what happened. She had had enough. The drugs, the late nights, not being home, ignoring her, she finally figured out it was time to dump me. The phone call from San Diego was the last straw. So she filed for divorce the next day. I did leave the house to her and I didn't ask her for anything for it. Getting divorced from her was probably one of the biggest mistakes of my life.

It didn't take long for me to get a bartender job at the Primavera Restaurant on the island. I worked hard and made some decent money. This was a high end place so I got some nice tips. On a typical Saturday night they would turn the tables two and half times. This is where I made the second biggest mistake in my life. One of the waitresses was hitting on me and we started dating. Like a dope I ended up marrying her. What a nut case! She made Alex Forrest in the movie Fatal Attraction look like Mother Teresa. This woman was a maniac. Almost immediately I was getting calls from the bank about overdrawn funds. And she would act like a raving lunatic when there was no money in the bank. Once, I got a call from the bank where she got access to my safe deposit box. Sure enough she cleaned out the box of money and jewelry. She would call my ex wife and demand money from her. She once took all my clothes out of the closet and sold them to a thrift shop. I had to take the distributor cap off the car when I was at work for fear she would steal the car and sell it. Needless to say, this marriage didn't last long. So, I got a divorce as soon as possible and was done with wife number three.

I stayed in San Diego a while working at the restaurant. I toned down the stealing for the most part. Every so often I would work with the maître'd and we would pocket some food checks but not much. I longed to get back to Vegas but I needed the heat to blow over for a while. One reason I wanted to get back was to watch my son grow up. I had a boy with the second wife and I thought it would be good to watch him grow up. So, after a few years I went back to Vegas. I got a dealer job. You guessed it. I was back downtown. This time I was at the Las Vegas Club. I needed to learn the game over again since they changed a lot of the odds payoffs. I worked the day shift at the Club for about a year.

I left all of my moves back in San Diego. I played the straight and narrow for a couple of reasons. First, I wanted to keep the job and I wanted to get a job at the Paris Hotel which was about to open. Secondly, the technology improved quite a bit so it was much easier to watch the dealers and the action on the table. The Paris Hotel opened and I was able to get hired there. The Casinos at this time became industrialized. It was now big business and it was being run by executives instead of the wiseguys. It made it kind of boring really. You often hear old and present dealers say it was better when the mob ran Las Vegas. In many ways it was. Back then you asked for a comp to the buffet or tickets to the show right there at the craps table when you were playing. The Pit Boss would write it out for you right then and there. Today, you have to have so many points on your player's card for them to give you any comps. In many cases, you have got to have a boat load of points to get a simple slip for the buffet.

It has really changed with the big businesses. What hasn't changed though is the skimming operation. They still do it but now it is done in a bigger way. Instead of walking into the count room which would be impossible to do today, they just take it off the top. How? They simply make up a category called consulting. Each year the casinos pay consulting fees of hundreds of millions of dollars to these consultants. The only thing is, there really isn't any consulting going on. What a great scam! They take their fee right off the top before all other expenses get paid just like the old skim. And who gets screwed in the end? The creditors and shareowners are the ones who end up with the short end of the stick. Why do you think all of these huge casinos right on the strip keep filing for bankruptcy?

And who do you think is getting the consulting fee? You guessed it, the mob. They are just more sophisticated today doing what they are good at. When the casino runs out of money due to these fictitious expenses, they just go back to the bank to get more loans. It is the old steak dinner trick. They take the bankers out for the steak dinner, the show and the strip club and the next thing you know they get a bigger loan. After all, it is not their money they are loaning out.

Meanwhile, my brother Paulie got black listed back in Atlantic City. Yes, they have a black book there as well. As you remember, he went to A.C. to train new dealers. He did it and did a great job at it. He noticed a lot of the customers were coming by bus. The buses would bring people in from the cities such as Philadelphia and New York City. The trip would last about six hours. Everyone would get a free buffet and ten dollars in quarters to play with and they got to look at the scenery along the AC Expressway and Garden State Parkway. There were literally hundreds of buses coming in each day.

Paulie partnered up with this other guy and they put on their own bus company. The way they would get paid would be head counts on the bus junket. They would report to the Casino how many people they brought in and they would get $25 per person. It was a pretty good gig. Only Pauli got greedy. He would start reporting they were bringing in 40 people where in reality it was only 30 or 35. Not only would they pocket the money for the phantom customers, they would keep the rolls of quarters and sell the buffet tickets for half price on the boardwalk. Greed always does it. The casinos started counting the people walking off the buses and realized he was over reporting. So, they fired him and put him in Atlantic City's Black Book. He couldn't get a job there so he came back to Vegas to deal again. And where did he have to start? That's right. Downtown.

I did get that job at Paris though. It was a legit job and I stopped using my old moves. Those days were gone. I did get divorced from the nut job in

California and met a 21 dealer at the Paris. We got married and raised her three kids from a previous marriage. I tried to live like a normal person. We stayed together for a quite a long time but eventually we got divorced. I guess I am not made out for marriage so I ended it with divorce number four.

The early years in Vegas were the best years in my life. The city was really wide open. We had the best parties, the best entertainment, the best looking women, the best restaurants, the best night life, the best wiseguys, and most of all, the most money. We had the nicest cars, the nicest clothes, nicest houses, the nicest pools, the nicest golf courses, etc. We had it all. I was never so rich as back then. Every dealer and casino employee was flush with cash. I was up to $250,000 in liquid assets. We could have anything and we did it at any time of the day. It was really a great time to be in Vegas. The Casinos never saw us coming. And to think we got away with as much as we did. ***They never saw us coming!***

Made in the USA
San Bernardino, CA
24 July 2017